Formative Assessment
FOR SECONDARY SCIENCE TEACHERS

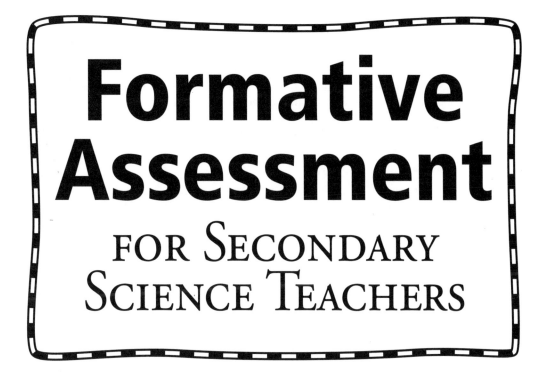

Formative Assessment

FOR SECONDARY SCIENCE TEACHERS

Erin Marie Furtak

CORWIN
A SAGE Company

For information:

Corwin
A SAGE Company
2455 Teller Road
Thousand Oaks, California 91320
(800) 233-9936
Fax: (800) 417-2466
www.corwinpress.com

SAGE Ltd.
1 Oliver's Yard
55 City Road
London EC1Y 1SP
United Kingdom

SAGE India Pvt. Ltd.
B 1/I 1 Mohan Cooperative
    Industrial Area
Mathura Road, New Delhi 110 044
India

SAGE Asia-Pacific Pte. Ltd.
33 Pekin Street #02-01
Far East Square
Singapore 048763

Printed in the United States of America

Library of Congress Cataloging-in-Publication Data

Furtak, Erin Marie.
Formative assessment for secondary science teachers/Erin Marie Furtak.
    p. cm.
Includes bibliographical references and index.
ISBN 978-1-4129-7220-8 (cloth)
ISBN 978-1-4129-7221-5 (pbk.)
    1. Science—Examinations, questions, etc. 2. Science—Study and teaching (Secondary)—Ability testing. 3. Science teachers—In service training. 4. Teacher effectiveness. 5. Educational tests and measurements. 6. Educational accountability. I. Title.

Q182.F87 2009
507.1'2—dc22   2009002815

This book is printed on acid-free paper.

09 10 11 12 13 10 9 8 7 6 5 4 3 2 1

Acquisitions Editor:	Dan Alpert
Associate Editor:	Megan Bedell
Production Editor:	Jane Haenel
Copy Editor:	Jeannette McCoy
Typesetter:	C&M Digitals (P), Ltd.
Proofreader:	Caryne Brown
Indexer:	Judy Hunt
Cover Designer:	Anthony Paular
Graphic Designer:	Karine Hovsepian

Contents

List of Figures and Tables

FIGURES

TABLES

Preface

The book you hold in your hand is the outcome of many years of research done by Richard J. Shavelson and his colleagues at the Stanford Education Assessment Laboratory (SEAL). In many cases, this research began before I even started teaching.

My work in formative assessment started during my time as a high school biology and earth science teacher. My education professors and school administrators always said that I needed to do formative assessment in my classroom. At that time, I thought that formative assessment consisted of pre-assessing students at the beginning of a unit and then doing quizzes and grading papers through each of my units to find out what they were learning.

When I went to graduate school, however, I had the good fortune of working for Professor Shavelson and SEAL's codirector, Maria Araceli Ruiz-Primo, and I learned that there was much more to formative assessment than I had previously known. During my years at Stanford, SEAL collaborated with researchers and curriculum developers at the University of Hawaii at Manoa on a study funded by the National Science Foundation (ESI-0095520) that tested Black and Wiliam's (1998) contention that formative assessment has a positive impact on student learning. This project was called the Romance Project and was initiated before I got to graduate school. Under the mentorship of Dr. Ruiz-Primo, my primary responsibility on the project was to assist in the development of formative assessments, to help train teachers taking part in the research, and to visit and communicate with the teachers as they enacted the assessments in their classrooms.

The study lasted three years, and we learned an immense amount about what formative assessment looks like in practice. For me, the study sparked my interest in what formative assessment truly was—not quizzes and assignments but a perspective on teaching that integrates students' alternative conceptions, good teaching practices, and research-based assessment techniques. I had the opportunity to present some of this work to teachers through the Center for the Assessment and Evaluation of Student Learning (CAESL) and to hear what they thought about it. Most of the time, the response was the same: Your research is interesting, but I want to hear about how I can use these assessment techniques and approaches in *my* classroom.

As a former teacher, I took that feedback to heart, reflecting on how my perspective had evolved through my work as a research assistant on the

Romance Project. I became committed to adapting all we had learned through our research into a resource for practicing teachers. I took the *Teachers' Guide to the Reflective Lessons*, the handbook written by SEAL for the research project, and adapted it into a workshop for teachers at a meeting of the Knowles Science Teaching Foundation and from there developed it into a book.

The work that is presented in this book is based on the research and curriculum development activities of a number of individuals: Rich Shavelson, Maria Araceli Ruiz-Primo, Carlos Ayala, and Yue Yin at Stanford, collaborating with Frank Pottenger, Donald Young, Paul Brandon, Rachael Jones, and Miki Tomita at the Curriculum Research and Development Group at the University of Hawaii. In addition, the book is based on the priceless experiences of the teachers in the Romance Project, who for the purposes of research will remain anonymous. These and the other teachers—and their students—featured in this book are identified only by pseudonyms, but without their openness and candor, this work would not have been possible.

Acknowledgments

F irst and foremost, I would like to thank Rich Shavelson, Maria Araceli Ruiz-Primo, and the Stanford Education Assessment Laboratory (SEAL), on whose research this book is based and whose mentorship has made me the researcher I am today. Rich Shavelson encouraged me to write this book and advised me in developing the outline on which it is based. Maria Araceli Ruiz-Primo, Carlos Ayala, and Yue Yin prepared the first version of a handbook for these types of formative assessments, and it was my later professional development sessions based on this handbook that provided the inspiration for this book. Jim Vanides thoughtfully wrote about our research group's experience with concept maps in an article in *Science Scope*, which helped me to structure one of the chapters in this book. Frank Pottenger, Donald Young, Paul Brandon, and Rachael Jones at the Curriculum Research and Development Group in Hawaii provided access to their curriculum materials to allow the first versions of many of these assessments to be developed. Many days spent scoring student work alongside Yue Yin ("What Would Melody Do?"), Noah Feinstein, Jeff Steedle, Miki Tomita, Marsha Ing, Colin Schatz, Gloria Banuelos, and Enrique Lopez helped me develop an eye for student ideas buried in long answers. Later, Jon Shemwell contributed with his critical perspective on formative assessment.

I also acknowledge the contribution of Mike Atkin and Misty Sato, whose perspective on developing science teacher knowledge for formative assessment helped me to see the value in the work I had done at Stanford as being more broadly applicable to the practitioner audience. I also deeply thank the teachers with whom I worked while a member of SEAL, whose experiences with formative assessment helped me to form my ideas about how to use them.

I thank Tina Limbird, Peggy Bleyberg-Shor, Alexander Morgan, and Charise Adams for providing me access to their students to develop some of the vignettes contained in this book, as well as Amanda Watson, who helped me develop and pilot some versions of the formative assessments. Susan Simpson, Courtney Trujillo, Patty Whitehill, Dori Walker, and Mark Perez also piloted some of the assessments contained in this book.

Sarah Roberts and Carolyn Kugler read drafts of the chapters closely and provided valuable feedback to increase the readability of the text. Victor Newberry, Mike Klymkowsky, and Laura Moin provided their valuable scientific expertise to make sure that the science on which the example assessments are based is solid. I also thank the reviewers whose insightful comments helped me to improve the quality of the manuscript.

As always, my work would not be possible without the unconditional love and support of my husband, Dave Suss, and my parents, Tom and Kay Furtak.

PUBLISHER'S ACKNOWLEDGMENTS

Corwin gratefully acknowledges the contributions of the following reviewers:

Stephanie Blake
Physics Teacher and Science
    Department Head
Parkview High School
Springfield, MO

Christine Brothers
Science Department Head
Falmouth High School
Falmouth, MA

Sharon Jeffery Cumiskey
National Board Certified Teacher,
    Early Adolescent Science
Plymouth, MA

Mandy Frantti
High School Physics and Math
    Teacher, NASA Astrophysics
    Educator Ambassador
Munising Public Schools
Munising, MI

Kathryn M. Glasheen
High School Science Curriculum
    Coordinator
Union County Public Schools
Monroe, NC

Michael Hoy
Science Department Chair
Neshaminy High School
Langhorne, PA

Susan Leeds
Science Department Chair
    and Teacher
Howard Middle School
Orlando, FL

Ellen Osmundson
Senior Researcher
CRESST, UCLA
Los Angeles, CA

Cheryl Schwab
Educational Consultant
Oakland, CA

Jo Topps
Regional Director
K–12 Alliance/WestEd
Santa Ana, CA

About the Author

 **Erin Marie Furtak** worked as a high school biology and earth science teacher in the public schools near Denver and has experiences in many other venues of education, including middle school, administration of professional development, and curriculum design. Her struggles to successfully implement inquiry-based teaching methods inspired her to pursue a career in educational research to make reforms more attainable for science teachers. After getting involved with a national research project where she designed and implemented computational science assessments, Erin decided to pursue a PhD so that she could have an impact on science teaching and learning beyond her own classroom. She studied curriculum and teacher education in the School of Education at Stanford University, writing a dissertation about teachers' enactment of inquiry-based science lessons in middle school. She then received the competitive German Chancellor Fellowship from the Alexander von Humboldt Foundation to study alongside educational researchers in Germany and spent 18 months living and doing postdoctoral research on middle school instruction in Berlin and Kiel. Erin is now Assistant Professor of Education specializing in Science Education at the University of Colorado at Boulder. She lives in Denver with her husband.

For Dave

1

What Is Formative Assessment?

WHERE ARE YOU GOING, AND HOW ARE YOU GOING TO GET THERE?

Imagine that you're going on a road trip. You started from Los Angeles in the early morning with the general idea of driving north to arrive in San Francisco by the afternoon or early evening. You've arranged to stay at your friends' house. You've been there before, so you have a general idea of where you're headed and what the house looks like, but you're not exactly sure in which neighborhood they live, and you don't have a street or house number for them either. Come to think of it, you're on Interstate 5 but haven't been paying much attention to where you've been, so you're not even sure how far away you are from where you started or where you're going.

Absurd as this scenario may sound, it's analogous to students' experiences in traditional science classrooms. Students know that they're in a science class, and they probably know their teachers are teaching a unit about some general concept with a title like "The Cell," "Force and Motion," or "The Ideal Gas Law." It's most likely, however, that these students don't have a clue as to what they're supposed to be learning, and they may also be challenged to let you know what they've done in class the past few days. It's not that much different from setting out in a car without knowing exactly where you're going and without a clear route for how you're going to get there.

In the road trip example, it's possible that you might find your way to your friends' house, but it's also likely that you would get lost and frustrated and end up spending the night in Sacramento after having made a wrong turn somewhere. It's the same way with students in a traditional classroom; some of them will end up learning what's expected of them, but others might end up walking away knowing something completely different from what you had intended.

A more realistic plan for a road trip would be to begin with the address of your destination. Then, after looking at a map, you would look at where you were starting from and make a plan for getting there. For instance, you might plan to leave Los Angeles at about 9:00 in the morning, taking US-101 to Interstate 5 heading north. You might plan a series of stops along the way to eat and stretch your legs. You would also plot out the series of directions you'd need to navigate in order to get from Interstate 5 into San Francisco and ultimately to your friends' house. You would thus have a clear idea of where you're going, where you are starting from, and how you're going to get there.

The process of formative assessment—the kind of assessment that takes place while learning is in progress—follows a similar procedure in providing a road map for student learning. Science teaching through formative assessment starts with setting a clear learning goal, making that learning goal explicit to your students, finding out what students know now, and then plotting an instructional course for students to reach the learning goal. Sometimes this process is also called classroom assessment or everyday assessment, but the basic point is the same: formative assessment is carried out by teachers in their own classrooms and is intended to help students reach learning goals.

This book is designed to help science teachers carry out formative assessment in their own classrooms—that is, setting a learning goal, finding out what students have learned so far, and making plans to help students meet that goal. It is built on an extensive research base developed over the course of the last 10–15 years that has established not only the impact formative assessment can have on student learning but also the relative effectiveness of different formative assessment strategies. The book will provide simple and clear explanations for what you can do to implement formative assessment in your classroom and will accompany these explanations with concrete examples from multiple grade levels and content areas.

WHAT IS FORMATIVE ASSESSMENT?

It's easy to think about assessment as something that's separate from everyday teaching. You finish teaching a unit, and students take a test to show what they learned. The state department of education interrupts your class for three days to see how well students in your school and district are progressing toward proficiency on the state standards. Juniors take the SAT for their college applications, and seniors take AP tests to get college credit.

These examples all have one thing in common: they are considered to be summative assessment or assessment that's intended to take place when instruction is finished to establish what students have learned. These assessments often have high stakes attached to them because they determine, for example, the kind of college to which a student can apply, the grade a student will get in a course, or the rating given to a school. Summative assessments serve an important purpose in finding out what students know—for example, finding out if students in a given class or school are meeting state standards. However, the high stakes attached to these tests have given the word *assessment* a bad name.

The problem with using only summative assessment in your classroom is that if you wait to assess your students when teaching is over, it's already too late. Returning to the road trip analogy, a summative assessment of your progress would simply state that you had arrived in Sacramento instead of San Francisco. It would have been much more helpful to know when you had made a wrong turn along the way so that you could have turned around and gotten back on the right road.

Fortunately, there's more than one kind of assessment. Assessment that takes place while learning is still in progress gives you information about what students know so that you can reteach a concept students have not understood, talk to individual students who may be off course, and better adapt your teaching so that all of your students can learn. *Formative* assessment is a kind of assessment that helps you modify teaching and learning while learning is in progress and can be thought of as assessment *for* learning and not *of* learning. It is called formative because it informs teaching and learning. It may sound a lot like a description of effective everyday teaching, and there's a reason for that; good teachers pay very close attention to what their students understand and constantly adjust instruction to help students learn.

Formative assessment follows the same procedure that you would use in driving from your home in Los Angeles to San Francisco. It consists of three steps that can be phrased as questions:

Where are you going?

Where are you now?

How are you going to get there?

These three questions comprise a process that is often called the formative assessment loop or the feedback loop; that is, the process of setting a learning goal, comparing that goal to what students currently know, and then giving students feedback to help them reach learning goals (National Research Council, 2001). Once you've set the learning goal, you can use a variety of formative assessment strategies like those presented in this book to find out what students know so that you can compare it to the goal. Then, if students have not met the goal, you can provide feedback in the form of questions, examples, or activities that will help them meet that goal. The formative assessment loop thus helps you to double-check that students have learned what you want them to know and allows you to make a contingency plan in the form of feedback that will help them to learn. This process is illustrated in Figure 1.1.

The first step involves deciding what students are going to learn during a lesson, a unit, or an entire course. Then, the teacher should tell students about those learning goals. The kind of learning goals that work with formative assessment go beyond simple lists of the different concepts students will learn. Goals that work well with formative assessment may come in the form of a question that will frame an instructional unit (e.g., What is an acid?) or can be criteria for what makes a good argument or a clear explanation. The goals can be stated explicitly or can be presented to students concretely in the form of exemplars that illustrate high-quality student work. Either way, it's important for students to know where they're going so that they can assess their own progress as they learn.

The second step involves finding out what students currently know as it relates to the learning goal. To do this, you need to have a way to get students to tell you what they actually understand, as opposed to rehashing what they think you want to hear, by asking open-ended questions, reading through student work, and listening to small-group conversations. It's important at this point to let students know they won't be graded on what they tell you because if you do, the students will focus on telling you what they think you want to hear rather than sharing their complex and often

Figure 1.1 The Formative Assessment Loop

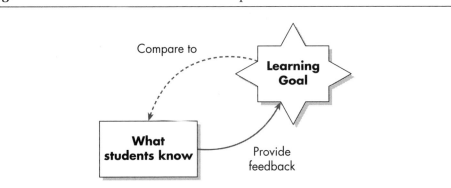

inaccurate ideas. Once you know what students think, you can compare what you found out with the learning goal and thereby identify what it is that students still need to learn.

The third step, and perhaps most important, is acting on this gap between what students know and what they need to learn. To help students reach learning goals, you need to give them some kind of feedback that points out inconsistencies in their thinking, connects what they know to more advanced concepts, or in some other way gives them information that will help them to improve their work. Feedback comes in a variety of forms: responding to students' questions, re-teaching important concepts that students have not understood, writing comments on their work, or encouraging them to set out steps for themselves to reach learning goals.

Over time, formative assessment loops can be connected together as you set increasingly challenging goals and help students to reach them through formative assessment. Each loop builds on the last, helping you to determine if students have truly met learning goals, so you can decide if students need more instruction to meet the present learning goal or are ready to move on to the next goal (Figure 1.2).

Figure 1.2   Multiple Formative Assessment Loops

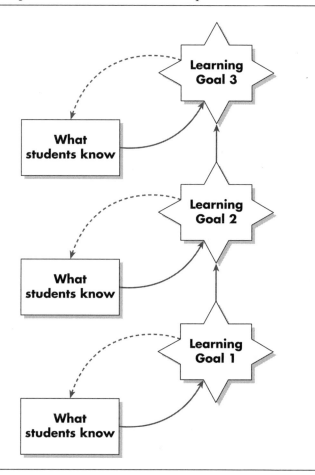

EFFECTIVENESS OF FORMATIVE ASSESSMENT

Sometimes, it seems as if educational researchers are looking for the *silver bullet* teaching method that will truly help all students to learn. There is probably no one approach that will ever be effective for all students, but research on formative assessment indicates that it has a larger impact on student learning than most other teaching interventions (Black & Wiliam 1998). In fact, in a review of more than 250 studies, Black and Wiliam (1998) found that low-achieving students had the greatest learning gains in studies of formative assessment. Black (1998) summarized the findings of the 1998 review into four features:

- Formative assessment will require new teaching practices and thus calls for significant changes in classroom practice.
- Students must be actively involved in their learning.
- For assessment to function in a formative manner, results have to be used to modify teaching and learning.
- Assessment has the potential to affect not only student learning but also motivation, self-esteem, and participation in self-assessment.

The finding that formative assessment is especially effective in helping lower-achieving students reach learning goals has important implications for increasing equity in education. Rather than sorting students into *haves* and *have-nots*, formative assessment can increase access to high-quality science education for *all* students (National Research Council, 2001; White & Frederiksen, 1998). Formative assessment helps you to set challenging learning goals and then provides the mechanism for helping your students get there. By paying very close attention to all students in your classroom and giving feedback to individuals aimed at helping them to reach learning goals, you can actively work to level the playing field for lower-achieving students, English language learners, and special education students in your own classroom.

After Black and Wiliam called the attention of the education community to the important role that formative assessment can play in helping students to learn, researchers have explored how teachers can enact formative assessment in their own classrooms. The rest of this book will adapt these research findings into concrete approaches to developing and enacting your own formative assessments in your classroom.

OVERVIEW OF THE BOOK

This book is organized into two main sections. The first section will describe in detail each of the three steps in the feedback loop of formative assessment.

Chapter 2 starts by describing the first step in the feedback cycle—setting learning goals. It includes planning sheets that will help teachers to identify and organize learning goals and then to determine where formative assessments can be embedded in units of instruction.

Chapter 3 discusses the second step in the feedback cycle—determining what the students know now. The chapter is an overview of teaching strategies and different kinds of questions that teachers can ask of their students to elicit their developing ideas and understandings.

Chapter 4 discusses the step in the feedback cycle that Black and Wiliam (1998) found positively impacts student learning: giving feedback to the students to help students close the gap between what they know and what they need to learn. It establishes the importance of giving students informational, nonevaluative feedback on their work both in discussions and in writing and then talks about the importance of modifying instruction to help students progress toward learning goals.

The second section of the book, which includes Chapters 5 through 9, presents in-depth descriptions of five different kinds of formats for formative assessments. These strategies will help to make concrete the different steps discussed in the first section of the book so that you can begin to develop your own formative assessments. Each strategy is described in the following ways: what it is, where to use it in a unit, how to develop it, and how to enact it in the classroom. Each chapter includes several examples of each kind of assessment, including a vignette of what the assessment looks like in action. The examples in these chapters are drawn from a range of grade levels and content areas.

Chapter 5 covers *Big Idea* assessments, which are basically short-answer questions that pose the question that frames your unit as a formative assessment. Students are encouraged to provide evidence and examples and to use diagrams or other representations to explain their thinking.

Chapter 6 describes *Concept Maps,* which are assessment tools in which students graphically represent the connections between different concepts.

Chapter 7 introduces *Predict-Observe-Explain* assessments, which are adaptations of demonstrations in which students predict what will happen in a given experimental scenario, observe what happens, and then write an explanation of why they think what they observed happened.

Chapter 8 talks about *Evidence-to-Explanation* assessments, where students use their conceptual knowledge to develop an explanation based upon a graph, table, or diagram.

Chapter 9 discusses *Multiple-Choice Questions* used for formative assessment purposes. It explains how multiple-choice questions linked to students' common ideas—accurate and otherwise—can help you quickly find out what your students know. Asking students to justify their choices provides you with more information about why they chose a particular answer.

The Resources section provides additional items for you to draw upon for more information about the assessments described in this book. It includes planning sheets, a complete list of references for the book, and a glossary of terms used in the book.

Let's get started!

PART I

Defining the Feedback Loop

Part I of this book will focus on the three steps in the feedback loop in-depth:

Step 1: Where are you going?

Step 2: Where are you now?

Step 3: How are you going to get there?

As we go through each of the three steps, we'll gradually build a planning process that can help you to develop formative assessments tailored to your own curriculum.

In the first step, deciding what you'd like students to learn, we'll consider the science content you're teaching, learning goals you want students to reach, what you want to know about student learning (the purpose of the assessment), and placement of the assessment in the unit.

In the second step, finding out what the students know now, we'll consider a range of simple strategies you can use in your everyday practice to get students to share their thinking. We'll also start thinking about actual assessment activities you can plan in advance and determine the different kinds of data that you can collect about student learning.

In the third step, providing feedback, we'll talk about the targeted student understanding, but more important, we'll talk about how to predict the possible alternative conceptions your students might have and how to anticipate the kinds of feedback you can use to help students move toward learning goals.

2

Step 1

Setting Learning Goals

Chapter Overview

- **The importance of setting learning goals**

- **What is a learning goal?**

- **Multiple types of learning goals**

- **Identifying science content**
  - **Starting from standards**
  - **Mapping a curriculum**

- **Bringing goals together: Planning for formative assessment**

THE IMPORTANCE OF SETTING LEARNING GOALS

When you walk into a classroom, you probably have some kind of goal in mind no matter what method of lesson planning you use. You plan to teach today about the Ideal Gas Law, and you have some textbook problems you'd like students to solve and maybe even a lab or activity in mind for students to complete. This plan consists of a general concept you want to teach (e.g., the Ideal Gas Law) and some activities for the students to do, but it does not have clearly articulated learning goals framing what your students will learn. Will your students need to memorize the formula $PV = nRT$? Will they use the equation to solve problems out of the textbook?

Will they be asked to research and explain kinetic molecular theory, or will they investigate the effect temperature has on the volume of a gas?

If you want students to develop specific abilities and understandings, you need to set clear goals for what you want them to learn. The goals then act as the destination, allowing you plan a clear route for how to get your students there. You can then develop a set of formative assessments that will tell you if students have reached the learning goals, giving you information about their progress in learning while you can still help them get back on the right path. This chapter talks about how to set and make explicit specific learning goals for your students as a foundation for conducting formative assessment in your classroom.

WHAT IS A LEARNING GOAL?

To start, I want to say that there are a lot of different ways to think about learning goals. Sometimes they are a general idea about a concept or topic a student will come to understand, other times they are overarching ideas that frame an entire course, and in still other cases, they can be exit outcomes for a school or state (Wiggins & McTighe, 2005). In this chapter, when I speak about *learning goals*, I mean simply what you would like students *to know and be able to do* at any point in instruction—whether it be the end of a lesson, unit, or course. Clear expectations for what students will know and be able to do will serve as the target for everything that comes afterward in formative assessment—getting your students to make their thinking explicit, comparing what your students know to the learning goal, and then looking for strategies and activities that can move students toward that learning goal if they're not there yet. Your learning goals are the pins on your map that mark the places you want to visit on your trip.

Let's unpack that phrase for a minute—*know and be able to do*. What students *know* refers to the understandings you want students to develop, including terms, facts, concepts, as well as more organized knowledge such as categories, principles, or theories (Furtak & Ruiz-Primo, 2008). In addition, what students know includes more organized and integrated understandings that allow students to apply principles or use explanatory models to approach a problem. This type of understanding is sometimes called *schematic knowledge* (Li, Ruiz-Primo, & Shavelson, 2006), such as a student's understanding of why it's colder in the winter and warmer in the summer.

What students *are able to do* involves skills, algorithms, techniques, and methods (Furtak & Ruiz-Primo, 2008). These can include procedures such as taking measurements and solving problems, as well as processes such as asking scientifically oriented questions or developing explanations from evidence collected in class and developing scientific habits of mind. This may include asking questions, building and testing scientific explanations, communicating ideas, using evidence to support arguments, and applying knowledge to new settings (National Research Council, 2001, p. 32).

Being specific about what exactly you want students to know and be able to do is the essential first step to creating effective formative assessments. While it may be tempting to focus exclusively on the simpler things that you want students to know, such as vocabulary and basic facts, formative assessment is probably better suited to developing integrated—that is, schematic knowledge—since these are involved with students' larger ideas about how the natural world works and involve alternative conceptions that are resistant to instruction. So if you focus your formative assessments only on simple facts, you'll miss out on the opportunity to find out what your students have learned so far and, more important, the chance to do something about it.

Goals that specifically state what students will know and be able to do have been shown to be more effective at capturing students' attention and increasing their interest in activities than vague goals. Making a learning goal explicit to students at the beginning of a unit is an important start because students need to internalize learning goals for them to be truly effective. The clarity and coherence of learning goals helps to increase students' feeling of support and competence during science lessons (Seidel, Rimmele, & Prenzel, 2005). To help students understand the criteria they are expected to meet, it's also useful to revisit your expectations for student learning multiple times throughout a unit, discussing and refining them to help students develop ownership of those criteria (National Research Council, 2001) and develop the ability to assess their own learning progress (Sadler, 1989).

MULTIPLE TYPES OF LEARNING GOALS

Obviously, setting just one learning goal for an entire unit is not enough. To carry out formative assessment as a part of a unit, you need to go beyond setting only one learning goal for students to achieve by the end of a given unit. As you plan instruction, you should have learning goals at every level: an *overarching learning goal* for an entire unit or course of study and *supporting learning goals* for every lesson and activity that your students will complete that build on each other to prepare your students to reach the overarching goal. In this way, you're planning out a continuum of what students will come to know—with their prior ideas and alternative conceptions at one end, the overarching learning goal at the other, and the supporting learning goals in the middle (see Figure 2.1). Continua like this are coming to be called learning progressions and form road maps for student learning of concepts in science (National Research Council, 2007).

An overarching goal is important because it will orient you and your students toward what you ultimately want them to learn. I have found it useful to phrase overarching goals as both statements and what are often called "big idea" questions. These questions help to organize the information contained in an overarching learning goal into a question to drive student inquiry during your unit. These questions help to "hold together related content knowledge" (Wiggins & McTighe, 2005, p. 66).

Supporting goals build on each other toward the overarching goal and big idea question for your unit, forming the steps that you will help your students climb as they come to know the science content you want them to learn. Identifying and articulating these goals will help make expectations explicit for you and your students. Then, for every step in the learning process that is essential to understanding the final goal, you should design a formative assessment so that you know before proceeding through the unit if students have or have not reached that goal.

Whether you're planning your own instructional unit or working with one that's already written, you need to have a set of clear learning goals to guide your teaching. In this chapter, we'll discuss how to identify the important science content your students will learn during a unit of instruction and how to translate that content into *big idea* questions, overarching learning goals, and supporting learning goals. Then we'll discuss how to decide where to place formative assessments in your unit and what the purpose of those formative assessments will be.

IDENTIFYING SCIENCE CONTENT

In the present era of accountability, what you teach in your own classroom is influenced by district, state, and national standards and is assessed by statewide tests that measure your students' progress toward those standards. Thus, the unit that you develop needs to be derived from standards

Figure 2.1   Supporting Learning Goals Forming the Steps Toward the
Overarching Learning Goal

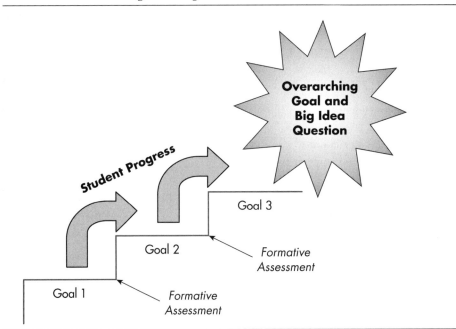

that are often densely packed with information and need to be rephrased as learning goals. In other cases, you will need to determine the learning goals for a packaged curriculum or textbook that was selected for you. In this section, we'll work through the process of setting overarching goals, big ideas questions, and supporting goals for these two situations—starting from standards or starting from a textbook or curriculum.

Starting From Standards

If you're designing your own curriculum, the content you will teach should come from the standards documents used at your school. However, standards are often densely packed with information and do not always lend themselves easily to developing learning goals. One of the most commonly used approaches to setting unit goals and planning curricula when you're starting with standards is the backwards planning approach introduced by Wiggins and McTighe in their book *Understanding by Design* (2005). Following this process, curriculum development begins by establishing what you want students to know by unpacking standards into learning goals, determining what will be acceptable evidence that students have reached those learning goals, organizing those goals according to their level of importance, and then planning activities that will build the understanding represented in that final goal.

The first step Wiggins and McTighe suggest is to identify the standards you will want to meet through instruction. However, standards are not so much goal statements as they are descriptions of the content students are supposed to learn. Take as an example this content standard for biological evolution for students in Grades 9–12 from the *National Science Education Standards* (National Research Council, 1996, p. 185), shown in Table 2.1.

Table 2.1 National Science Education Standard for Biological Evolution

---

Science Content

- Species evolve over time. Evolution is the consequence of the interactions of (1) the potential for a species to increase its numbers, (2) the genetic variability of offspring due to mutation and recombination of genes, (3) a finite supply of the resources required for life, and (4) the ensuing selection by the environment of those offspring better able to survive and leave offspring.

Source: National Research Council. (1996). *National Science Education Standards.* Washington, DC: National Academies Press, p. 186.

This standard helps us out by stating a clear understanding that students should know: species evolve over time. Looking across the other important ideas that recur within the standard, it is clear that the process of natural selection described in the four steps listed is the mechanism by which evolution works. So we can add this piece to what the standard has provided to come up with the overarching learning goal: The students will come to know that species evolve over time through the process of natural selection. Simply rephrasing that statement as a question leads us to our big idea question that will drive student inquiry in the unit.

Table 2.2 Overarching Learning Goal and Essential Question for Natural Selection Unit

Overarching Learning Goal	Big Idea Question
The students will come to know that species evolve over time through the process of natural selection.	How do species change over time?

Once you've got the overarching learning goals and big ideas you'd like students to learn, the next step is to sequence those understandings to build on one another toward the overarching learning goal. To do so, think about what students need to know before learning the next idea so that each of the understandings builds on the one before. Envision standing at the bottom of a staircase where the top represents the goal you'd like students to reach, and the steps represent the understandings students need to develop in order to reach those goals. The standards are intentionally stripped-down, so this process of creating the *staircase* may take some rewording based on your knowledge of the subject.

Taking the natural selection example, we can look back at the standard to see that the understandings students should learn are listed in four discrete steps. By thinking about these concepts as a story, we can reword as we go so that the individual goals make more sense in succession with each other. The first thing students need to know is that populations are capable of exponential population growth and that there will be variation among members of any population. However, since there is a finite amount of resources available in any natural environment, only those offspring that are well suited to the environment will survive and reproduce. These statements comprise four supporting goals for the unit. The goals are shown in Figure 2.2.

Since each of these supporting learning goals builds on the last, it's important that you know your students have understood each goal as you teach the unit. Otherwise, you may reach the end of your unit with several students still stuck on understanding one of the supporting goals you thought you had already taught. This means that for every supporting learning goal, you should develop a formative assessment so that you can collect information that will help you know how to tailor instruction to help all of your students meet the overarching goal.

The natural selection example was relatively straightforward thanks to the writers of the standards, who clearly laid out the understandings students needed to develop. It was also an illustration of a "the students will come to know" goal. However, learning goals are not only what you want

Figure 2.2 Supporting Learning Goals for Natural Selection Unit

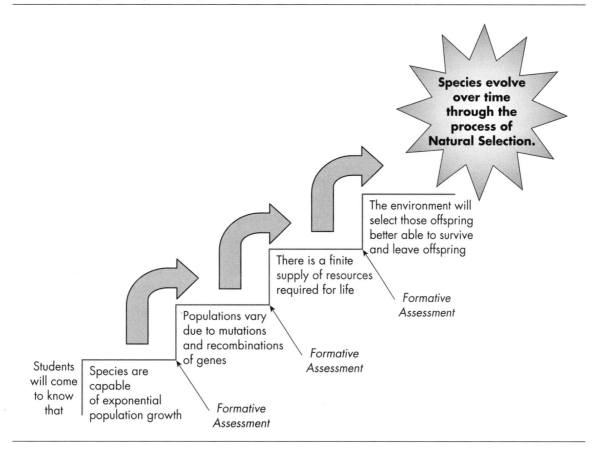

students to know but also to be able to do. Let's go through a quick example of a "students will be able to" goal.

With the exception of the standards that deal with students' abilities to engage in scientific inquiry, most of the content standards are phrased in terms of what students will come to know. This means that you'll have to take matters into your own hands and interpret the standards into things your students will actually be able to do. Let's take Content Standard F from the standards for earth and space science in Grades 5–8 as an example, in Table 2.3.

Table 2.3 National Science Education Standard for Earth and Space Science

Science Content

- Lithospheric plates on the scales of continents and oceans constantly move at rates of centimeters per year in response to movements in the mantle. Major geological events, such as earthquakes, volcanic eruptions, and mountain building, result from these plate motions.

Source: National Research Council. (1996). *National Science Education Standards.* Washington, DC: National Academies Press, p. 160.

This standard is stated in a manner lending itself all too easily toward a *know* overarching goal: "The students will come to know that lithospheric plates . . . ." However, we want to push our students to engage and interact with the content they are learning, so merely memorizing information isn't enough. To go beyond this know goal, the standards suggest that an activity for students learning about lithospheric plates could involve them plotting the locations of geologic activities such as earthquakes and volcanoes.

Table 2.4 Overarching Learning Goal and Essential Question for Earth Science Unit

Overarching Learning Goal	*Big Idea Question*
Students will be able to identify patterns in geologic activities such as earthquakes and volcanoes.	Where do earthquakes and volcanoes happen?

To be able to reach this overarching goal, students need to have some basic knowledge of what earthquakes and volcanoes are, and they need to be able to plot the locations of these geologic events on a world map. These two supporting goals form the steps leading to the overarching goal, and you can develop a formative assessment at each step to make sure students have the necessary foundational understandings in order to meet that overarching goal.

Figure 2.3 Supporting Learning Goals for Earth Science Unit

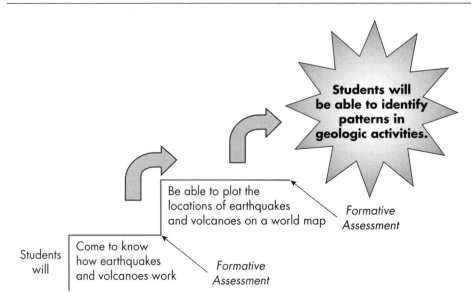

Mapping a Curriculum

If you've already got a textbook or curriculum you're working with, your task in setting learning goals is a bit different from what we did above. By curriculum, I mean not just a textbook by itself but a programmed set of lessons or activities from a textbook or curriculum that are oriented around learning goals. For example, if you're using one of the inquiry-based curricula like the Full Options Science System (FOSS; Lawrence Hall of Science, 2000), you're provided with a set of questions for students to respond to that are already phrased as questions. For example, in the Variables curriculum, learning goals are phrased as essential questions such as:

- How does a scientist learn about the world?
- What are the steps involved in scientific inquiry?
- What is a variable?

These questions both create a need to know in students by asking something that they can't answer, as well as serving as goals for students' investigations. If they are constantly reminded of the question they're trying to answer, they know where they're going and have an overarching theme to which they can relate their developing understandings.

In other curricula, you may need to read carefully through the provided sequence of activities to look for the overarching goal toward which the curriculum is oriented. A helpful approach when you're analyzing a preexisting curriculum is to make a list of the activities that students will be completing and the supporting learning goals for each of those activities. Writing this information down will force you to read the activities more carefully and will help to focus on what the curriculum designers intended for students to learn.

For example, in a study in which researchers and curriculum developers collaborated to embed formative assessments into a preexisting unit, Ayala et al. (2008) mapped out the major activities and learning goals in the first unit of the Foundational Approaches to Science Teaching (FAST) curriculum (Pottenger & Young, 1992). This first unit, titled The Properties of Matter, takes students through a series of investigations to help them develop a density-based explanation of sinking and floating. Going through the process of analyzing the goals and activities of each individual investigation helped the curriculum developers, teachers, and researchers rethink the activities being taught and to develop an overarching question to guide the unit. A summary of the investigations is shown in Table 2.5.

The sequence of activities in the unit is a succession of investigations into the properties of mass, volume, and density and how those properties affect whether an object will sink or float in water and other liquids. After a careful analysis of these goals and activities in the FAST curriculum, Ayala et al. (2008) determined that a big-idea question to frame the unit might be, "Why do things sink and float?" (Table 2.6).

Table 2.5 Summary of Investigations and Learning Goals From FAST: The Properties of Matter

Lesson	Activity Title	Student Activities	Learning Goal
1	Liquids and Vials	Observing a buoyancy anomaly	Making scientific observations; testing predictions
2	Sinking a Straw	Adding mass to a straw and measuring its depth of sinking	Predicting the number of BB's required to sink a straw to a chosen depth
3	Graphing the Sinking-Straw Data	Creating a graph of mass versus depth of sinking	Representing data in graphs
4	Mass and the Sinking Straw	Sinking straws to depth based upon total mass	Increasing mass means a straw will sink more
5	Sinking Cartons	Sinking cartons of different sizes with equal mass	Predicting the depth to which a carton will sink
6	Volume and the Sinking Cartons	Calculating the volume of cartons	Calculating the displaced volume of a carton
7	Floating and Sinking Objects	Calculating the mass and volume of objects	Predicting the displaced water of floating and sinking objects
8	Introduction to the Cartesian Diver	Experimenting with a Cartesian diver	Discovering how a Cartesian diver works
9	Density and the Cartesian Diver	Finding the density of a Cartesian diver	Finding the density of a diver at different depths
10	Density of Objects	Calculating the density of objects	Finding the density of floating and sinking objects
11	Density of Liquids	Finding the density of liquids other than water	Finding the density of liquids
12	Buoyancy of Liquids	Finding the relationship between buoyancy and density	Understanding relative density

Table 2.6 Overarching Learning Goal and Essential Question for FAST: The Properties of Matter

Overarching Learning Goal	Big Idea Question
The students will come to know how the properties of mass, volume, and density affect whether an object will sink or float.	Why do things sink and float?

Once you've decided on the goal that you want students to reach, the next step is to map the progress your students are expected to make during the unit—that is, to determine which of the learning goals in your curriculum form the steps that will help students reach the over-arching goal. If you've generated a list of learning goals from a pre-existing curriculum, the sequencing has already been done for you; the activities that meet each learning goal have already been put together in an order that is conducive to helping students learn. However, in order to decide where to place formative assessments, it's important to go through the sequence of lessons to look for the points where students need to develop particular understandings if they are to reach the ulti-mate learning goal.

Wiggins and McTighe (2005) suggest a useful tool for determining which content is most important for students to come to know (i.e., the big ideas), what it is important for students to know and be able to do, and what students just need to be familiar with. Their tool, which I call a *bull's-eye*, helps you to pull out overarching and supporting learning goals from the rest of the information that's contained in a unit (see Figure 2.4).

Going back to the example of the research done by Ayala et al. (2008) on the FAST curriculum, the unit summary shown in Table 2.6 was analyzed to determine the important points in the unit where it was essential students understood a particular big idea before moving on to the next

Figure 2.4   Wiggins and McTighe's "Bull's-Eye"

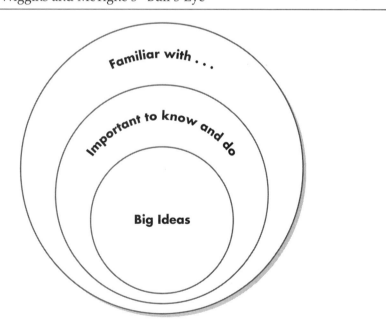

Source: Adapted with permission from *Understanding by Design* (2nd ed., p. 71), by Grant Wiggins and Jay McTighe. Alexandria, VA: ASCD. © 2005 by ASCD. Used with permission. Learn more about ASCD at www.ascd.org.

investigation—what students need to know and be able to do if they are ultimately going to be able to respond to the overarching question for the unit. By looking through the list of students' activities and the list of goals for each activity, Ayala et al. (2008) determined that while there were independent learning goals for each of the investigations, some were more important than others; for example, understanding the impact of mass when volume was controlled and then volume when mass was controlled was more important than knowing the number of BB's it might take to sink a straw to a particular depth (Figure 2.5).

The goals from the know-and-be-able-to-do circle on the bull's-eye can then be placed in sequence to form the staircase that will help students be able to answer the big idea question for the unit (see Figure 2.6). Since the supporting goals form the route your students will follow to reach the overarching learning goal and big idea question, you need to assess each of these goals through a formative assessment to make sure students are making adequate progress. In this way, you'll be able to collect valuable information about what your students are learning as you go through the unit, which in turn allows you to plan instruction to meet students' needs.

Figure 2.5 Bull's-Eye for Sinking and Floating Unit

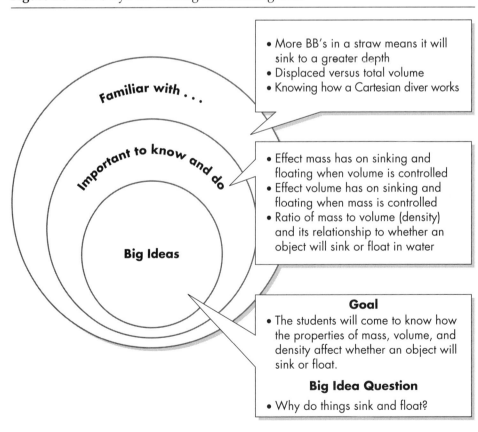

Figure 2.6   Supporting Learning Goals for Sinking and Floating Unit

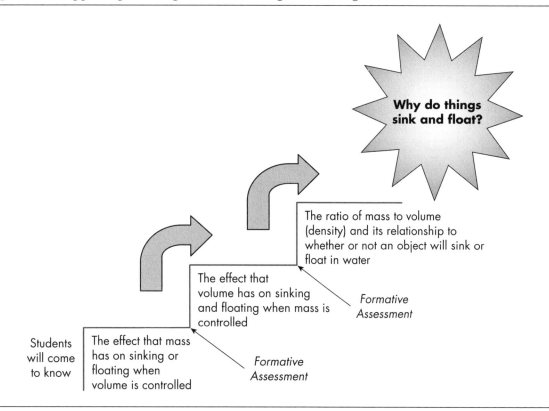

BRINGING GOALS TOGETHER: PLANNING FOR FORMATIVE ASSESSMENT

Regardless of whether you're writing a curriculum entirely on your own or are developing formative assessments to embed in a curriculum, it's important to keep track of your planning process as you go. Planning Sheets A and B in the Resources lay out the three-step process for setting learning goals that we've gone through in this chapter:

Step 1: Identify standard(s) for the unit and summarize activities in unit

Step 2: Unpack standard(s) into overarching goal and big idea question for unit

Step 3: Write supporting goals that will help students reach the overarching goal

Once you've got this information, you can develop a formative assessment for each supporting learning goal. Table 2.7 illustrates how the science content, overarching learning goal, big idea question, and each supporting learning goal can be written out to help you plan each formative assessment.

Table 2.7   Planning Process for Natural Selection Formative Assessment

Science content	Species evolve over time. Evolution is the consequence of the interactions of (1) the potential for a species to increase its numbers, (2) the genetic variability of offspring due to mutation and recombination of genes, (3) a finite supply of the resources required for life, and (4) the ensuing selection by the environment of those offspring better able to survive and leave offspring.
Overarching learning goal	The students will come to know that species evolve over time through the process of natural selection.
Big idea question	How do species change over time?
Supporting learning goal	The students will come to know how new variations arise due to mutations and recombination of genes.

We can go through the same process for the earth science and sinking and floating units, illustrated in Tables 2.8 and 2.9.

Table 2.8   Planning Process for Earth Science Formative Assessment

Science content	Lithospheric plates on the scales of continents and oceans constantly move at rates of centimeters per year in response to movements in the mantle. Major geological events, such as earthquakes, volcanic eruptions, and mountain building, result from these plate motions.
Overarching learning goal	Students will be able to identify patterns in geologic activities such as earthquakes and volcanoes.
Big idea question	Is there a pattern to the places earthquakes and volcanoes happen?
Supporting learning goal	The students will come to know how earthquakes and volcanoes work.

Table 2.9 Planning Process for Sinking and Floating Formative Assessment

Science content	Properties and changes in matter, Content Standard 1 for Grades 5–8: A substance has characteristic properties, such as density, a boiling point, and solubility, all of which are independent of the amount of the sample (NRC, 1996).
Overarching learning goal	The students will come to know how the properties of mass, volume, and density affect whether an object will sink or float.
Big idea question	Why do things sink and float?
Supporting learning goal	When given the density of an object, students will be able to predict whether or not that object will sink or float in a given liquid.

Whether you're starting from scratch in developing your own curriculum or working from a textbook or curriculum, the planning process we've gone through will help you to get the information you'll need to plan formative assessments in the following chapters.

3

Step 2

What Do the Students Know Now?

Chapter Overview

- Where are the students now?

- Strategies for making students' thinking explicit

  o Establishing a classroom environment conducive to formative assessment
  o Asking open-ended questions
  o Teaching strategies

- Determining what counts as evidence

- Planning for formative assessment: Finding out what students know

---

WHERE ARE THE STUDENTS NOW?

In Chapter 2, we discussed the importance of setting clear learning goals for instructional units and then making those goals explicit to students so that they know where they're going. This establishes the first step in the formative assessment loop. Once those goals are set, the next step is to find out what your students know with respect to that goal so that you can determine how far they are from meeting the learning goals you've set for them. This chapter is about the different approaches you can use to find out what your students know.

To truly find out what your students are thinking, you'll need to go beyond traditional approaches such as asking a question, getting a response, and then saying whether the response was right or wrong. Mehan (1979) called this approach "I-R-E"–style teaching. His finding, confirmed in more recent studies (Cazden, 2001), was that two-thirds of all interactions between teachers and students follow the same basic pattern: teachers *Initiate* by asking a question, the student *Responds*, and then the teacher *Evaluates* what the student said. This approach to teaching assumes that student responses are either right or wrong and does not give value to the great range between these two extremes. Students' ideas rarely map exactly onto what we expect them to say, and if they do, there's plenty of evidence to suggest that they're just parroting what the teacher said rather than processing what they learned for themselves.

So be prepared—when you start asking students to tell you what they know, you're going to hear a lot of different, unexpected responses. Take, for example, the ways that middle school students think about volume as it relates to density. The basic principle of a density-based explanation of sinking and floating is that if an object has more mass per unit volume than water, it will sink, and if it has less, then it will float. However, consider the different responses students gave in several different classes when their teacher asked them to give an explanation about why things sink and float:

- "When you have more volume, the mass spreads out more."
- "If things are more compact—like packed together instead of spread out—they'll sink."
- "Isn't volume the space that something takes up?"
- "[It depends on] the weight of the object and amount of trapped air inside the object."

These responses all contain elements of the correct response but are at the same time representative of students trying to use their own words and ways of thinking to explain a complicated scientific concept. A teacher waiting for a particular response might look at all of these responses as being wrong, but a teacher with a formative assessment perspective informed by clear learning goals oriented toward in-depth understanding should see these as being rich pieces of information about where students are with respect to learning goals.

Let's look more closely at two of these responses to see what information they contain about what these students know.

- "When you have more volume, the mass spreads out more."

This statement is actually a quite sophisticated statement of the inverse relationship between density and volume. The student has stated that when there is more space in an object, the mass can be more spread out, making the density lower overall.

- "If things are more compact—like packed together instead of spread out—they'll sink."

This student is expressing a very common colloquial way of describing density as compactness. Things that are very dense have a lot of mass packed together in a smaller space, whereas things that are less dense had mass that is more spread out over a larger volume.

This collection of student responses is intended to help you start to see all the complex information contained in student ideas and why it's important to really find out what they know. They are all productive in the sense that they can be built on to help students develop more sophisticated scientific understandings (Smith, diSessa, & Roschelle, 1993). Let's look at some specific strategies that you can use to get students to share ideas like these.

STRATEGIES FOR MAKING STUDENTS' THINKING EXPLICIT

While every student is filled with his or her own explanations of the natural world, most won't readily share them with you. Students are socialized after years of school to look for the correct answers and to please their teachers and tend to hide their misunderstandings in case they will receive bad grades for it. They have years of experience saying the *scientific* answer right back to their teacher while they hold on to their own alternative conceptions about how things happen. In order to really find out what your students are thinking, you have to first create a classroom environment in which they feel safe to share their ideas with you and then use strategies that will really get at their thinking.

Chapters 4 through 9 of this book will present five different formats for formative assessment that can help you get at your students' ideas, but in order to use these strategies, you'll also need to develop a repertoire of strategies and questions to use with them. In this section, we'll talk about creating a classroom climate in which students feel free to share their ideas and listen respectfully to their peers. Then the section will include strategies and questions you can use to better understand your students' thinking.

Establishing a Classroom Environment Conducive to Formative Assessment

When you do formative assessment in your classroom, you're asking students to do a scary thing: tell you (and often the whole class) what they really think, even if it's wrong. In fact, the effectiveness of formative assessment depends on the teacher's finding out accurate information about the students' knowledge. Unfortunately, the culture of many classrooms makes doing so very difficult for students. For formative assessment to work, students need to feel safe in order to reveal what they know and believe, in a setting where ideas—not individuals—are discussed, compared, criticized, and revised. For this to happen, you need to create a community of scientists in your classroom who are focused on figuring out the answers to scientifically oriented questions and who will consider any idea plausible until it is subjected to the standard of scientifically collected evidence.

The first, and perhaps most important step, is to avoid grades on formative assessments. Butler (1987; Butler & Nisan, 1986) found that when students were given grades and feedback on their work, they paid attention only to grades and not to feedback. Furthermore, if students know they are being evaluated, they will do everything they can to give you the information they think will get them a good grade rather than telling you what they really think. If you must give points or a grade, do it based on completing the assignment or on participating in a group or class conversation rather than on their actual ideas.

Next, it's important for you as the teacher to put value on students' effort rather than allowing them to think that some students are just smarter than others. If students attribute their successes to their effort, they are more likely to keep trying rather than give up when they are confused or make a mistake. You can reinforce this by building students' autonomy and complimenting them on trying hard or letting them know they are making progress (Stefanou, Perencevich, DiCintio, & Turner, 2004). Table 3.1 includes these and a few more "do's" and "don'ts" for creating a class-room environment conducive to formative assessment.

Table 3.1   Creating a Classroom Environment Conducive to Formative
Assessment: Do's and Don'ts

Do Let Students	*Don't* Let Students
Know that learning is more important than grades.	Feel that they are ranked.
Share their understandings with the class even though their ideas might be wrong; questions or confusion can actually contribute to the learning of the class.	Feel that only correct answers are preferred in class.
Know that all students can learn if they make an effort.	Feel that some students are smarter than others.
Know that it's okay to make mistakes; what's important is to learn from them.	Feel that they always do worse than others because they are not smart enough.
Know that science is interesting, valuable, and important.	Feel that science is boring.
Connect what they learn with what they observe in everyday life.	Concentrate only on the content of the curriculum.
Know everybody can learn well if only they try hard.	Feel that they are incapable of learning some difficult topics.

Source: Adapted from Stanford Education Assessment Laboratory. (2003). *Teacher's Guide to the Reflective Lessons.* Unpublished manuscript.

Asking Open-Ended Questions

I'll state the obvious: If you want to know what students really think, "yes" or "no" questions or questions that can be easily answered with one or two words are not enough. In order to really get at what students are thinking, you need to ask more authentic, open-ended questions that are genuine requests for information about student thinking. Cazden (2001) calls questions that teachers ask when expecting a right or wrong answer *instructional* questions and questions that teachers couldn't answer themselves *real* questions. Whereas an instructional question might entail stating a scientific term and asking students to define it, a real question could be asking for a prediction or an explanation of why something happened.

Instructional questions will keep you in the traditional mode of teaching that is pervasive in classrooms. To find out what your students know, you need to ask open-ended questions that get students to share their thinking, respond to each other, and clarify their ideas. A collection of this type of question is shown in Table 3.2.

Don't worry about memorizing all these questions; just pick a few that would work well with the goals of your lesson plan and ask them over and over to multiple students. Jot these down in your lesson plan book or on a piece of paper you can keep with you when you're teaching. Before you start a class discussion or go around to individual students or small groups, just glance at these questions to remind you of what you'd like to ask.

Keep in mind that these are going to be tough questions for students to answer, and responses to them won't just pop out of students' mouths. Give students plenty of time to think before you ask anyone to share his or her answer. The basic rule of thumb for wait time is eight seconds, and sometimes counting this out in your head can help you realize how rarely we as teachers wait long enough for students to respond. If you're talking to the whole class, ask students to raise their hands before shouting out answers so that all students have a chance to be heard. You might see a few hands shoot up right away when you ask the question, but keep waiting until you get a larger sampling of students with something to say before calling on anyone. Wait time gives more students a chance to think what they might answer themselves rather than cutting short their thinking time by calling on the fastest or boldest student first.

Teaching Strategies

So far, we've talked about conditions for creating a classroom environment supportive of formative assessment as well as types of questions that you can ask students to get at what they are thinking. How do we embed these questions into instructional strategies? Later in the book, I'll present five specific formats for formative assessments, but regardless of what format you use, it's helpful to mix things up by using a lot of different strategies to get students working with each other and reflecting on their ideas. Sometimes, you'll want to get students to share their ideas quickly just so you know what they are thinking; sometimes you'll want them to

Table 3.2 Open-Ended Questions for Formative Assessment

Question Type	Function	Description or Examples
Getting at students' ideas	Predicting	What is your hypothesis? Have you seen/done anything like this before? What is your prediction? What is your "theory"? What do you think is going to happen? Why?
	Exploring	What kind of experiment can you do to support your argument? What can you do to find out? What kind of evidence would you need?
	Observing	What did you observe? What surprised you?
	Interpreting data	What do you know from this graph? Why do you think this happens?
	Evaluating	What is your conclusion? Is it the same as what you expected? Why or why not? Do you plan to change your "theory"? If so, why? How?
Responding to students	Clarifying	Can you explain this more? What do you mean by [word (e.g., density)]? Could you give me an example? What evidence do you have to support this?
	Asking for evidence	How do you know? What evidence supports your ideas? Why do you think it is right or wrong? Why do you disagree or agree with them?
Promoting discussion	Getting students to argue and defend their ideas	What do you think about what [student name] just said? Do you agree or disagree? Why? What other ideas do you have? How will you persuade others? Does that argument make sense to you? Why/why not?
Reflecting	Summarizing/ reviewing	What have we learned today? What is the difference between what we learned today and what we learned last week? If your parents ask you what you have learned today in science class, what will you tell them? How would you explain to a third grader what you learned today in class?
	Self-evaluating	What is still unclear to you? What confuses you? What do you think you know after today's class?

evaluate their own work; and other times, you'll want them to argue their ideas and come to a consensus. For each of these purposes, there are several teaching strategies; the list shown in Table 3.3 includes eight possible teaching strategies that work well with formative assessments.

Strategies That Elicit a Range of Student Ideas

Sometimes you just want to know what your students are thinking about a particular topic or concept—for example, when you're about to start a unit or after students have completed an investigation. At these times, the following strategies are useful for quickly getting a range of students to share their thinking with the class. The first two—vote and class survey—are perhaps the simplest and fastest way to get a bunch of student ideas out without a lot of processing or discussion. The second two—think-pair-share and table conference—will give students more of an opportunity to talk about ideas in pairs or as a group before sharing with the whole class; the investment of time will be worth the in-depth responses your students will provide.

• *Vote.* When you're doing an assessment to which there is a limited range of answers (e.g., whether an object will sink, float, or have neutral buoyancy), give students time to write down their own answers and then ask students to vote on which one they chose. Write down the tally of student responses on the board or give students sticky notes and ask them to come to the board to *cast their vote* by placing the note beside the answer they agree with. Once all student responses have been tallied, ask students to give reasons for choosing different answers or reasons why they did not

Table 3.3   Teaching Strategies for Formative Assessment

Purpose of Assessment	Teaching Strategy
Eliciting a range of student ideas	Vote
	Class survey
	Think-pair-share
	Table conference
Promoting self-assessment	Self-review
	Peer-review
Promoting argumentation and consensus	Table consensus
	Jigsaw and debate

Source: Stanford Education Assessment Laboratory. (2003). *Teacher's Guide to the Reflective Lessons.* Unpublished manuscript.

choose particular answers. By asking your students to choose among a limited number of options, this strategy will help you get a very quick overview of what students in your class think.

• *Class Survey.* One way to quickly hear a range of student ideas on an open-ended question is to have groups or individuals share their ideas in response to the question. Write these ideas down on the board so that all students can see them and then invite students to discuss them. Use this strategy with caution, however, because students with incorrect or unclear ideas are less likely to share them with the whole class (Furtak & Ruiz-Primo, 2008). Taking the time to take a look at students' written work after doing a class survey will give you a more accurate picture of what all of your students know.

• *Think-Pair-Share.* This time-honored teaching strategy works very well as a formative assessment starter to get students to share their ideas. Pose a question and then give students a few minutes to think about the question and write down their ideas. This first step is essential if you want students to think about what they know before talking to someone else. Once all students have something written, ask them to turn to the person beside them to discuss their thoughts for several minutes. While students are talking to each other, walk around the room to listen to what students are saying to each other so that you have an overview of what all of your students are thinking. After a few minutes, ask a few pairs to share their discussion with the class so that the students can hear what other pairs talked about. Taking the intermediate steps of having students think independently and then talk to a partner in a low-risk setting will help them to process their responses before joining a whole-class conversation and will ultimately lead to a richer discussion than would be possible if you posed a question to the whole class.

• *Table Conference.* If you don't want to have a whole-class discussion, use smaller groups as places for students to talk to each other about an issue of confusion, misunderstanding, or debate. Simply pose a question or scenario to students as a whole class and ask them to discuss the different sides as a small group. Before releasing students to their small groups, ask the groups to ensure that each student has an opportunity to speak, and encourage students to talk about each other's ideas rather than making the discussion personal. In this kind of discussion, students should talk about a range of ideas and discuss their strengths and weaknesses. During a table conference, walk around to different tables and listen in on each discussion for a few minutes.

Strategies That Promote Self-Assessment

Research indicates that asking students to self-assess helps them to internalize learning goals, which in turn can increase their learning and motivation (Reeve & Jang, 2006; Sadler, 1989). When you would like your students to evaluate their own progress toward learning goals, provide them with the criteria by which their work will be measured or an exemplar of student work and ask them to gauge their own progress with respect to the criteria or exemplar.

- *Self-Review.* To help students internalize the criteria that have been established for evaluating their work, you may ask students to write their own responses to a question and then compare their own work with the criteria or an example. Ask students to revise their work in response to seeing the criteria. In this way, you help students learn to look for and correct their own mistakes.

- *Peer-Review.* Ask students to write down their responses to a given question and then have students trade papers with their classmates. Hand out a sheet of paper to each student that explains the answers or criteria for their work and then ask them to give detailed feedback to their peers on what is missing from their response and how they might improve their work. For example, if students have been asked to write an explanation and support it with evidence, students might read each other's work and give comments on whether or not evidence had been provided and speak to the quality of that evidence. You may decide to conclude the activity by returning students' work and asking them to respond to the comments provided to them by their peers. This strategy has the double advantage of having students internalize criteria by commenting on the work of other students, which can positively impact their motivation to learn (e.g., Reeve & Jang, 2006), while at the same time motivating students to revise their own work in response to those criteria (Sadler, 1989).

Promoting Argumentation and Consensus

The National Science Education Standards emphasize that students' ability to argue scientific ideas and formulate scientific explanations on the basis of evidence are essential elements to engaging students in the process of scientific inquiry (National Research Council, 1996). Asking students to argue ideas and come to a consensus in small groups or as a whole class can give students an opportunity to engage in argumentation and can also help students learn how to evaluate the quality of arguments based on available scientific evidence.

- *Table Consensus.* While a table conference gets students talking about a range of ideas, the table consensus strategy forces students to come to a decision about the question or scenario at hand. If you already know the range of ideas in your class based on some of the quicker formative assessment strategies, asking students to build consensus around a particular idea will force students to convince each other of the strength of their own position, and you'll be surprised at how animated some groups will get during their discussions. Encourage students to base their decision making on the quality of scientific evidence supporting the different ideas or conclusions they are discussing. You can also use this strategy when there is a question, confusion, or misunderstanding. After allowing students time to talk in their small groups, ask table groups to share their process as well as their final decision with the whole class.

 • *Jigsaw and Debate.* Divide students into groups representing different ideas and let them meet for several minutes to discuss the ideas and the evidence that supports them. Then number students off in these small groups and reassemble them into jigsaw groups, where an individual with each idea is present in each group. Ask students in the jigsaw groups to debate the different ideas and the evidence in support of them. The advantage of having students meet in same-idea groups first is that they can decide upon the best evidence to present in favor of their idea before being confronted with a debate. It may be useful to ask students to argue in favor of an idea different from their own, to encourage them to have more perspective and to make the debate less personal.

When you're deciding which strategy to use, think about what you've done so far, how much time you have, and how you'd like to group your students. Figure 3.1 organizes these eight strategies according to the level of grouping and the amount of time they take. For instance, the Think-Pair-Share strategy can be completed in just a few minutes and groups students individually, in pairs, and as a whole class; the table consensus strategy takes longer and involves students working in groups and then as a whole class, whereas the self-review strategy works primarily with students as individuals and can be completed fairly quickly. Regardless of which strategies you prefer, mix things up so that your students have multiple ways to show you what they know.

Figure 3.1   Formative Assessment Teaching Strategies Organized by Time Involved and Level of Grouping

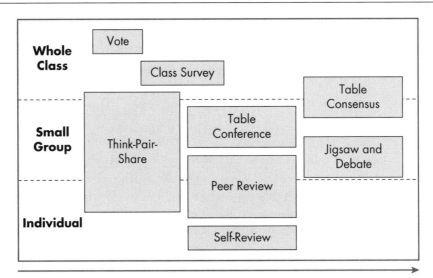

DETERMINING WHAT COUNTS AS EVIDENCE

Before proceeding to the final step of the feedback loop, it's worth mentioning what counts as evidence in support of student ideas during formative assessment. In many of the strategies and questions above, I mentioned that students should evaluate the quality of ideas based on the scientific evidence collected in class in support of those ideas. This contention is based on the National Science Education Standards, Benchmarks for Scientific Literacy, and other science education reform documents that argue that students' explanations in science should be supported by evidence.

But what counts as evidence? This is a complicated question, which has many different answers depending on whom you ask—scientists, philosophers, historians, or educators. The science education community generally states that evidence should be empirical—that is, based on observation in a scientific setting, usually an in-class investigation. Accordingly, what Marisol did on her summer vacation last summer, what Jeff saw on TV, or what Lin heard from a friend does not count; therefore, it is a good idea to hold a conversation with the class about what will count as evidence during classroom discussions and to set standards that will be applied to what students say.

Beyond these planned formative assessments, you need to be open and responsive to the possibility that as you teach, opportunities will arise for formative assessment. Identifying these moments can be as simple as paying attention to students' expressions and realizing that, if half the class looks perplexed, it might be a good chance to stop teaching and reflect on what you've done so far to determine where some students may have gotten lost. You may also find opportunities to stop and ask direct questions of students as you're circulating around the class during group activities to check students' understanding.

PLANNING FOR FORMATIVE ASSESSMENT: FINDING OUT WHAT STUDENTS KNOW

In the previous chapter, I introduced a planning sheet on which you could write out information relevant to the goals you set for each formative assessment you will design: the standards you are going to address, your overarching learning goal, the big ideas question, the related supporting goals, the assessment purpose, and the point in the unit where that assessment will be placed. In this chapter, we discussed a number of questions and strategies that you can use to find out what students know. To continue that planning process as you decide how you're going to find out what students know, think about the purpose of your assessment, the placement of the assessment within the unit, the assessment activity you're going to write, as well as the data to be collected about student learning. At this point, you may just jot down questions and strategies that you'd like to use to get at students' thinking. In Chapters 5 through 9, I'll present five specific formats for formative assessment that will help you use these questions and strategies to get at students' ideas. Table 3.4 includes the next steps in the planning process.

To illustrate this next planning step, let's take a minute to go through the examples for the natural selection and sinking and floating units that we started in the last chapter.

In the natural selection example, we worked with the learning goal that students would come to know: how new variations arise due to mutations and recombinations of genes. A way to conduct formative assessment would be to ask students a question about where they think variations in species come from, why they think so, and what evidence they have in support of their ideas. Students may get together in groups and conduct a table conference to share their ideas with each other. This plan is summarized in Table 3.5.

We can go through the same planning process for the earth science unit with the second supporting goal, which deals with students' ability to accurately plot the locations of earthquakes and volcanoes on a world map; without being able to do so, students will not be able to look for a pattern in their locations (Table 3.6).

Turning to the sinking and floating unit, we set the goal that students would come to know that density is a property of a material and is independent of its shape or size. An activity to help students share and then test their ideas would be to present students with several blocks made of the same material, each one with a different shape and size. Asking students to vote on whether or not each of these blocks will sink or float in

Table 3.4 Planning Process for Step 2: Finding Out What Students Know

Assessment purpose	Reason that a formative assessment is being developed for this supporting learning goal (e.g., to find out quickly what students are thinking, to test students' ideas, or to force students to come to a consensus on an explanation)
Placement in unit	Location in unit where assessment will be placed; description of the activities that come before and after it
Assessment activity	Description of the actual activity that students will be doing for the formative assessment or questions and strategies you'll use to get at students' thinking
Data to be collected about student learning	What kind of information will be collected about what students know, and how will it be collected and analyzed by the teacher?

Table 3.5   Example Step 2 Planning Process for Natural Selection Unit

Assessment purpose	Teacher needs a quick overview of student ideas with respect to where new variations come from.
Placement in unit	Prior to the formative assessment, students will have learned about how exponential population growth means that individuals of a species always produce more offspring than can be supported by the environment. After the formative assessment, students will explore how some individuals will better fit into the environment than others and how those that are a better fit will survive and reproduce.
Assessment activity	Teacher will ask students: Where do you think variations in species come from? Why do you think so? What kind of evidence do you have to support your ideas? Place students in groups to collect all student ideas through a table conference.
Data to be collected about student learning	Teacher will circulate to groups during assessment activity to listen to students' different ideas, and then will ask each group to present to the class all the ideas at their table. Teacher will write down ideas on the board and cluster similar ideas together.

Table 3.6   Example Step 2 Planning Process for Earth Science Unit

Assessment purpose	The teacher needs to know that students have mapped locations for earthquakes and volcanoes accurately before talking about patterns in where they occur.
Placement in unit	In the middle of the unit, before discussion of patterns in locations of earthquakes and volcanoes and lithospheric plates.
Assessment activity	Peer and self-review: students will plot a set of earthquake and volcano locations on a world map and then will be provided with a criterion map on which these locations are plotted. Students will be encouraged to check their peers' work and their own work, and when they have plotted a location incorrectly, discuss why they may have done so before correcting it.
Data to be collected about student learning	Teacher will circulate around classroom and check the location of certain earthquakes (e.g., Northridge or Loma Prieta) and volcanoes (e.g., Mt. Fuji or Mt. Kilauea) to see that they have been plotted correctly.

water will be a way to find out how many of them know that the density of a material is constant, such that what happens to one block will happen to all the other blocks (Table 3.7).

Now that we've talked about where you are going (setting learning goals) and where your students are now, it's time to turn to the final— and most important—step in the formative assessment loop in the next chapter.

Table 3.7   Example Step 2 Planning Process for Sinking and Floating Unit

Assessment purpose	To determine whether students understand that sinking and floating can be predicted based on a comparison of the density of the liquid and the density of the object; if the density of the object is greater than the liquid, it will sink; otherwise, it will float.
Placement in unit	The assessment will take place toward the end of the unit, after students have measured the density of sinking and floating objects and identified trends in whether they sink or float in water. After the assessment, students will find the density of various liquids, then sink and float objects in these liquids.
Assessment activity	Given a set of blocks of the same materials but cut into different shapes and sizes, students will predict whether they will sink or float in water. Students vote on what they think will happen and then participate in a class discussion where they explain why they voted the way they did.
Data to be collected about student learning	Teacher will tally student votes for the different predictions and will listen to the students' reasons for making their prediction.

4

Step 3

Anticipating Feedback

Chapter Overview

- Feedback: Plotting a learning course for students
  - Defining feedback
  - Four types of feedback

- Anticipating students' alternative conceptions

- Providing feedback
  - Verbal feedback
  - Feedback in writing
  - Modifying instruction

- Anticipating feedback

- Putting it all together: Planning the steps in the feedback loop

---

FEEDBACK: PLOTTING A LEARNING COURSE FOR STUDENTS

So far we've talked about the first two steps in formative assessment: setting learning goals and finding out what the students know so far. While these two steps help students know where they're going and where they are, they only set up the conditions for the third step: feedback. Feedback is the most important step in the formative assessment loop. It is the action that helps students move toward learning goals. Providing descriptive feedback to students has been shown to be the most essential of the three steps in the formative assessment loop to helping students learn (Black & Wiliam, 1998; Sadler, 1989). Feedback comes in many forms and can be as simple as asking students a question to push their thinking further; in other cases, feedback can entail reteaching an important concept that students have not yet understood. Feedback is ideally tailored to each student, and that's what makes it the most complicated and challenging of the three steps in formative assessment. In this chapter, we'll talk about what feedback is, how to plan the feedback you will provide by anticipating what your students know, and how to provide feedback in discussions, in writing, and by modifying instruction.

Defining Feedback

Research has shown that teachers' most common responses to students are right or wrong evaluations of what they have said (Cazden, 2001; Mehan, 1979). An example of this kind of exchange might look like the following:

Teacher: What is Newton's second law?

Student: *F* equals *MA*.

Teacher: Yes, you've got it.

In contrast to this exchange, feedback that is part of formative assessment should go beyond telling students they are correct or incorrect. Instead, the feedback you provide students should give students information about what they have done and then provide them with a path to reach the learning goal. As discussed in the first chapter, feedback is the step in formative assessment that has a positive impact on what students learn (Black & Wiliam, 1998).

Feedback should provide information to the students about the gap between what they know and what they need to learn. Through feedback, students gain information about the strengths and weaknesses of their performances so that they can maintain those aspects that are of high quality and focus their efforts on those in need of improvement. This feature of feedback is an essential element of effective formative assessment so that students come to see their work not as right or wrong but as part of a continuum of growth toward increasing quality or degree of expertise (Sadler, 1989).

Dylan Wiliam (2007) uses the analogy of the advice a softball coach might give to a player to illustrate feedback that is formative in purpose. A coach telling a pitcher that her slider pitch is not cutting away from the batter as it approaches the plate has identified a problem but has given her no information on how to fix it. However, a coach who tells the pitcher that she needs to modify the placement of her fingers as she grips the ball gives her pitcher specific information needed to get the pitch working correctly.

Four Types of Feedback

There are several types of feedback that you can provide to students. Hattie & Timperley (2007), in a review of research on feedback, identified four different kinds of feedback: feedback on the task or product, feedback aimed at processes, self-regulation, and personal feedback.

Feedback about a *task or product* is the most common type of feedback, where the teacher tells the student what has been left out and what needs to be included, such as, "You should use the scientific word for that," or "You forgot to label the *y*-axis."

Second, Hattie and Timperley argue that providing feedback *"aimed at the process used to create a product or complete a task"* (p. 90) is ultimately more effective than providing information about a task alone since it reinforces students in learning the methods that will help them improve their work in the future. For example, middle school students often have trouble with putting the proper scale on the *x*- and *y*-axes when making a graph. Evaluative feedback would involve simply telling students how to number each axis, but feedback aimed at the process of making a graph might involve talking with students about what is represented on the axis and how every interval needs to have the same value.

The third category of feedback is *self-regulation*, where you provide students with information about how to monitor their own learning progress and establish their own routines. Examples include teaching students strategies about how to keep track of their own engagement in an activity and helping them to be aware of their own process of learning.

The final category is *personal feedback* that is directed at the effort students are putting into the task. An example might be to tell a student, "You're making good progress because you've been able to finish this lab report," or "I can tell you're working very hard because your work today is much more accurate." It's important to distinguish between this kind of effort-related feedback and that which is directed at the student themselves (e.g., "You're smart" or "Good girl"), which may actually be counterproductive in helping students to reach learning goals.

I explain these four categories to highlight and emphasize that feedback need not always be task-related but can also include information about processes, self-regulation, and the learner's progress. There's no formula for when you should use each different type of feedback; rather, keep these categories in mind and try to use them all frequently to ensure the feedback you're providing students is the kind that will increase their learning.

ANTICIPATING STUDENTS' ALTERNATIVE CONCEPTIONS

Research in science education has shown that students have prior ideas about scientific phenomena. Anyone who has seen the Annenberg Foundation's *Private Universe* videos, in which Harvard University graduates provide inaccurate and illogical explanations for why it is hotter in the summer than in the winter, has felt surprise (and perhaps frustration) at the inability of our educational system to address and do something about students' alternative conceptions. Part of the reason that alternative conceptions are so persistent is that teachers often ignore them, or in other cases, try to show students how they are incorrect rather than helping students adapt their unscientific ideas into more accurate ones (Smith, diSessa, & Roschelle, 1993).

One of the most important functions of formative assessment is to get students to share these prior ideas or alternative conceptions with you so that if needed, you can do something about them. However, the alternative conceptions that students share are often phrased in nonscientific terms and are difficult to recognize so that if you are standing in front of a class and need to give feedback quickly, it can be quite difficult to know how to help students when alternative conceptions come up in conversation.

One of the best ways to proceed when students share alternative conceptions is to anticipate some of the prior ideas that students might have about a particular topic they are learning and to think about what students who have those ideas might need to know, an activity they might do, or a question you might ask, so that when you do formative assessment, you'll be prepared for what they say. However, newer teachers might not know exactly what their students might be thinking and what kinds of alternative conceptions they might hold—after all, that's the purpose of formative assessment in the first place!

The best place to go for information on alternative conceptions is to the bibliography *Students' and Teachers' Conceptions and Science Education*, maintained by Reinders Duit at the Leibniz Institute for Science Education at the University of Kiel in Germany (Duit, 2007). This database was started in the 1970s by Helga Pfundt and is an index of research about students' everyday ideas about science. You can download this database for free at http://www.ipn.uni-kiel.de/aktuell/stcse/stcse.html. The database also keeps track of research into teaching strategies for those students who have particular misconceptions. The database is available either as an EndNote file or as a rich text document, and using keywords in the database you can find a lot of information to help you build these questions.

However, it will also be the case that over time you will learn about the common ideas and alternative conceptions that students have as you listen to what they say during formative assessment situations. Pay attention to patterns that you see in what students say and jot down what you remember so that next year, you'll have a longer list of what students might say and a better idea of what to tell them. In the next sections of the chapter, we'll talk specifically about what the feedback you provide actually constitutes.

PROVIDING FEEDBACK

You can provide feedback to students in a variety of ways, including telling them something directly in a discussion, small group, one-on-one interaction, writing comments on their work, or modifying instruction for an entire class. Regardless of the way that you provide feedback to students, it's essential that the feedback contain specific information about how students can improve their performance.

Verbal Feedback

Perhaps the simplest and most straightforward way to respond to information you gain about what students know is to say something to them right away, whether it's one-on-one, in a small group, or to the whole class.

The first thing to keep in mind when giving verbal feedback is to not give students a simple right or wrong reaction to their answer but instead to give them detailed information about what they said and, if they have not yet reached learning goals, how to improve their performance. If students are correct, you can reinforce your learning goals or criteria by telling them *why* their response was good. In a whole-class setting, this can also help other students better understand the standards to which they are being held so that they may begin to self-assess. For example, you could say to a student, "Your explanation is well supported by the evidence we collected in class," or "You used several scientific terms in your answer; way to go!" Such responses highlight what students did well rather than just telling them they were right.

Feedback in Writing

If you collect information about what students know on paper, it can also be appropriate to give students feedback directly in writing. This approach to providing feedback can be incredibly time-consuming, but research indicates that it's a good way to motivate students and help them learn.

Thanks to the work of Ruth Butler, we know quite a bit about how the information provided to students on written work impacts their performance. Butler found that students who received comments on their written work were significantly more interested in the activity than those who received grades or no feedback. The comments group also scored higher on a measure of attribution of effort. In terms of students' performance on the task, the comments group scored significantly higher than the other two groups (Butler & Nisan, 1986).

Thus, if you provide feedback to students in writing, be sure not to provide grades but to take the time to give students information about how they did and how they can do better next time.

Modifying Instruction

The approaches of providing feedback in discussion and in writing are more targeted to individual students; however, information from formative assessment can also be used to plan and modify entire units of instruction.

Planning Instruction

If you decide to ask students a series of questions at the beginning of a unit as a preassessment, for example, you can use the information that you collected to plan instruction so that it specifically targets the different ideas held by students in your class.

Take this example from teaching a physics lesson about force and motion (Harlow & Otero, 2005). To find out what the students knew about force and friction, a teacher asked students what would happen to a toy car if they pushed it on a flat surface and then let it roll forward. The students responded overwhelmingly that, after a little while, the car would slow down. The teacher asked a few students to explain why they thought the car would slow down, anticipating that they would have the common alternative conception that the force "runs out" of the car. To the teacher's surprise, students mentioned several different ideas, including that gravity would have an effect on the car, or the car would be slowed down by the cracks in the floor. Another student simply said, "It just stops."

A common response to these different ideas would have been for the teacher to tell all of the students that they were wrong or perhaps to focus in on the student who believed that the car was somehow slowed down by the floor—the beginning of an idea of force and friction. However, the concept of feedback goes beyond evaluation and means that the teacher would provide each student with information about what they might think to get a more scientifically accurate understanding of how the car moved.

This teacher instead planned an activity in which students investigated the motion of the car on increasingly rougher grades of sandpaper so that students would come to see that the rougher the surface on which the car is traveling, the more quickly the car slows down. Students collected and graphed data from the investigation and then presented their explanations to the class. In each group, students were able to relate the fact that the bumps on the sandpaper were responsible for the car slowing down, talking about how the bumps "pushed" against the car as it moved.

In this example, the investigation itself is a form of feedback designed explicitly to help students see the cause for the car slowing down. Through the course of the investigation, students were able to observe that friction is a force that somehow pushes against the car, making it slow down. This understanding represents progress compared to the students' various initial ideas, and over the course of the unit, the teacher came to introduce the words *force* and *friction* as a continuous process of moving students toward learning goals.

Reteaching Important Lessons and Concepts

In other instances, teachers may find that, through formative assessment, students have not made the conceptual progress they had anticipated and choose to reteach a particular lesson. The example of two teachers involved in the Foundational Approaches to Science Teaching (FAST) research project serves as an important illustration of this point.

These two teachers had each been asked to enact a formative assessment halfway through the sinking and floating unit. The formative assessment was placed in the unit after students had measured the mass and volume of sinking and floating objects and created a graph to look for a relationship. The purpose of the formative assessment was to find out if students understood that objects with a ratio of mass to volume that was greater than one-to-one would sink, and others would float. The first teacher—we'll call him Mr. Nolan—rushed through the investigation so quickly that students did not have time to complete their graphs. When Mr. Nolan carried out the formative assessment, he found that only a few of his students were able to identify the one-to-one ratio of mass to volume in floating objects that should have been represented in the graph, but he chose to move on anyway. Mr. Nolan concluded the lesson by telling students what he wanted them to know, and then started the next investigation.

The second teacher, Ms. Schafer, was holding a discussion about the data when she realized that students had taken inappropriate measurements during the investigation, looking at displaced volume rather than total volume, thereby generating data that would not help move students toward an understanding of density. Rather than move on, Ms. Schafer decided to take the time to conduct the investigation again, this time making sure that students made measurements of total volume instead of displaced volume. Perhaps not surprisingly, when all was said and done, Ms. Schafer's students learned more in the unit than Mr. Nolan's students.

In some cases, reteaching an entire lesson might not be the best approach; information from formative assessments might simply lead you to reinforce a procedure or concept with students at the beginning of the next class. Either way, it's important to pay attention to what students know and adjust what you do in class accordingly.

ANTICIPATING FEEDBACK

This chapter began with a discussion about how difficult it is to provide feedback, then suggested that anticipating students' common responses was an important step. Unfortunately, there's no "silver bullet" phrase that you can always use when you're providing feedback. That's why I haven't provided a lot of specific examples to this point; the feedback you provide to students is by necessity specific to the student to whom you are speaking, containing details about that student's work.

However, if you have learning goals in mind and have done a little research on what students' ideas are likely to be, you can informally plan out some feedback that you could provide to students during formative assessment. This step may seem cumbersome, but anticipating feedback when you have the time and mental space is much better than waiting until you're in the thick of things in the classroom to think of what to say. Having even a few planned feedback responses for each of your lessons can help you improve your teaching and move students toward learning goals.

Since feedback is specific to what it is that you're teaching, I'll show you how to plan feedback responses by continuing the examples we've looked at the in the last two chapters. First, let's talk about the information necessary to anticipate feedback.

Since feedback is the loop-closing move that helps students reach toward learning goals, the first piece of information you'll need to look at is the learning goal that you've set. Then, write down all the probable responses or alternative conceptions that you expect students might have. By comparing these possible responses with the learning goal, you can begin to imagine some examples of feedback you might provide to students with those ideas—whether it's verbal or written or even a learning activity or example you could use to help students reach learning goals (Table 4.1).

Table 4.1 Planning Information for Feedback

Supporting learning goal	The scientifically accurate explanation or understanding to be elicited by the formative assessment
Probable student alternative conceptions	Listing of students' common prior ideas and alternative conceptions based on teacher's prior experience or research on the topic at hand
Feedback ideas	Summary of the next steps the teacher may take for each of the alternative conceptions listed above

Let's take a look at the evolution example that we started working with in the previous chapters. Students are expected to learn that new variations in individuals arise at random as a result of mutations and recombinations of genes through mating; however, when asked where new variations come from, students often say they are caused by the environment. Focusing students in on the random genetic processes that lead to mutations, as well as diagramming out how genetic changes in populations can occur over time, are both feedback strategies that can help students move toward learning goals. These steps are summarized in Table 4.2.

These feedback ideas are just a start, of course. The first time you carry out a formative assessment in your classroom, jot down some ideas students may have shared that you hadn't anticipated, as well as some of the feedback you provided if it was different—or more effective—than what you had planned. In Chapter 6, you'll see how another evolution formative assessment designed to assess a different learning goal was carried out in a science classroom and the revisions the teacher made after using it.

Table 4.2 Anticipating Feedback for the Natural Selection Example

Supporting learning goal	The students will come to know how new variations arise due to mutations and recombination of genes.
Probable student alternative conceptions	Students often think that changes in the environment cause changes in organisms; that is, organisms actively adapt to their environment.
Feedback ideas	Ask students to explain genetically how the changes in organisms arise and the randomness of mutations. Draw a diagram showing how a mated pair of individuals can produce offspring that vary among themselves and then talk about which of those offspring are more likely to survive and reproduce. Carry the diagram down for several generations so that students can see how the population changes over time as a result of selection, not environmentally induced changes.

The earth science example from the previous two chapters builds on students' understanding of how earthquakes and volcanoes work. These ideas should have been developed in previous science classes, but a science teacher would be remiss not to revisit these important concepts (Table 4.3).

Table 4.3 Anticipating Feedback for the Earth Science Example

Supporting learning goal	Students will be able to plot the locations of earthquakes and volcanoes on a world map.
Probable student alternative conceptions	Students may not understand how to read latitude and longitude or how they are represented on a map; for example, what N and S for latitude mean with respect to the equator, and what E and W for longitude mean with respect to the prime meridian. As a result, students may not be able to accurately plot the locations of earthquakes and volcanoes.
Feedback ideas	When students have an incorrect location, ask them to go through their process of identifying where the earthquake or volcano occurred so that you can see how they came to plot the event in that location. Tell them, "I hear a mistake in how you plotted that event," and focus them in on looking for E or W with longitude and N and S for latitude. If they are still confused, model the process of plotting a different event and then ask them to try the incorrect one again, following the same procedure.

Now let's take a look at the sinking and floating example. The learning goal we set in Chapter 2 had to do with students understanding density as a property of a material, independent of shape or size. However, students often think that by cutting a material into pieces or by manipulating a material into a different shape, its density can also be changed. To address these alternative conceptions, focus on talking about what the word *density* means and then on taking measurements and making observations of materials when their size or shape has changed (Table 4.4).

Table 4.4   Anticipating Feedback for the Sinking and Floating Example

Supporting learning goal	Students will come to know that density is a property of a material and is independent of its shape or size.
Probable student alternative conceptions	Students often believe that density will change when the shape or size of an object is changed.
Feedback ideas	Using blocks of the same material and cut into different shapes and sizes, have students measure mass and volume and then calculate density. Help them to see that, for a given material, changing the shape or size changes the mass and volume in equal proportions, and therefore the density—the amount of "stuff" in an object— stays the same.
	Do a demonstration with students where you show them how a piece of soap will sink in water. Cut the soap and then ask students what will happen to each piece of soap. Once students see that no matter the size of soap cut, it will still sink, talk about what density is and focus on how changing the shape or size will not impact its density and, therefore, whether it will sink or float.

As with the evolution example, a formative assessment for the same sinking and floating unit that we explored above is shown in action in Chapter 7.

PUTTING IT ALL TOGETHER: PLANNING THE STEPS IN THE FEEDBACK LOOP

Now that we've discussed all three steps in the feedback loop across the last three chapters, it's time to put these steps together to plan for formative assessment. I've included a blank planning sheet in the Resources that you can use to plan each of your formative assessments once you've identified learning goals for your unit.

While Chapter 3 discusses some different strategies for getting at what students know, the coming chapters will present to you five different formats for formative assessment: Concept Maps, Evidence-to-Explanation assessments, Predict-Observe-Explain, Multiple Choice, and Big Ideas. Each type of formative assessment helps you get at a different kind of learning goal, and each chapter will speak very specifically about how each type of formative assessment works and how to write and enact each. Each chapter then presents two ready-to-use formative assessments as examples, each time going through the planning process talked about in Chapters 2 through 4.

PART II

Formats for Formative Assessment

The first three chapters in this book have presented each of the three steps in the formative assessment feedback loop. Each chapter has contributed elements to create a Planning Sheet that will help you as you design your own formative assessments.

The remaining chapters in Part II will present five different formats for formative assessment that you can adapt to fit your curriculum and implement in your classroom. These chapters build on the planning process presented in Part I as they explain each type of formative assessment, discuss where and how to use the formative assessment within a unit of instruction, and present examples and vignettes of the formative assessments in action in real classrooms. The examples and vignettes cover multiple content areas and grade levels within the range of secondary school.

Something you won't find in any of these chapters is an answer sheet because to look for a *correct* answer defeats the purpose that formative assessment is supposed to serve. You're not just looking for a right answer but for the range of student understandings on the path to that right answer. Thus, it's more important to plan out in advance what those intermediate understandings look like than to focus on the answers. The Planning Sheets that accompany all of the example formative assessments in these chapters contain much more information than you would find in an answer sheet, and you can use them to help you anticipate the kinds of student responses your students might share with you, as well as the type of feedback you could provide.

The next five chapters are organized according to the complexity of the process that goes into creating them. We start with Big Idea Questions, a type of open-ended response, and then move on to Concept Maps, Predict-Observe-Explain assessments, and Evidence-to-Explanation assessments, winding up with multiple-choice questions.

5

Big Idea Questions

WHAT IS A BIG IDEA QUESTION?

It's common to name units after the central topic or concept being taught; for example, a biology unit might be on "Evolution" and a physical science unit might be about "The Structure of the Atom." However, science education reformers are suggesting that teachers design their units to answer driving questions that organize students' activities and focus students in on the big ideas to be learned (American Association for the Advancement of Science, 1990, 1993; National Research Council, 1996; Wiggins & McTighe, 2005). These questions then become a guide for student inquiry during the unit, as well as a kind of formative assessment in themselves.

The big idea question is simply a way of focusing on the most essential part of the content in the unit, framing it as a "take-away" message and packaging it as the answer to a question. Thinking this way, our unit on Evolution could be designed to answer the question, "How do species change over time?" Similarly, a unit on atomic structure might ask, "Why are nuclear reactions so powerful?"

Units structured around big idea questions gradually build the student knowledge necessary to answer the question by the end of the unit. Using these questions *throughout* the unit, however, helps to focus the students on the ultimate learning goal and provides formative assessment information to the teacher at the same time. Asking students to provide short answers to the big idea question helps you to gauge their progress toward answering the question that is framing your unit.

WHEN SHOULD I USE BIG IDEA QUESTIONS IN MY UNIT?

A great feature of big idea formative assessments is that they are appropriate to use anywhere in a unit. Use them on the first day of a unit to engage students in the question to find out what your students already know about the topic or what they would like to find out. Use them in the middle of a unit to see if your students can use what they have learned so far to answer the big question or to reorient them on the real question you want them to be able to answer at the end of the unit. If your students are using science notebooks in your class, you can even have them write their responses into their notebook and then periodically reread and, if necessary, revise their answers to examine what they've learned so far.

Another advantage of big idea formative assessments is that their outcome space—that is, the area in which they write their response—is totally unstructured, so students can draw diagrams or pictures, write sentences, or represent their answer in whatever way they think is best. In this way, students are invited to demonstrate their understanding in a format of their choice.

HOW CAN I DEVELOP MY OWN BIG IDEA QUESTIONS?

A big idea question should frame important concepts in the context of a question that is of general interest. Wiggins and McTighe (2005) call these "topical essential questions," arguing they can frame units of study or even entire courses. Big idea questions should take students "beyond the specific content in a provocative and transfer-rich way" (p. 118), or to put it more simply, big idea questions are unifying concepts and help students to see how the content that they are learning can be applied to many other areas. To generate big idea questions, Wiggins and McTighe suggest you start with national or state standards, identify the important concepts that recur, and then make them the basis of your question. They provide the following example from the Michigan Science Standards (p. 119):

> *Life Science:* All students will apply an understanding of cells to the functioning of multicellular organisms, including how cells grow, develop, and reproduce.

Topical Essential Question: How can we prove that cells make up living things?

If you are preparing a handout, write your big ideas question and then leave the space below the question blank rather than making lines so that students aren't forced to respond in sentences but can also use diagrams or other representations. The orienting questions in the planning sheet below will help you to think further about how to implement the formative assessment, what kinds of responses you might expect, and what to do about them (Table 5.1).

Table 5.1 Planning Process for Big Ideas Formative Assessments

Step 1: Setting Learning Goals	
Science content	What standards-based understanding will your big idea be based on? What is the big idea that your unit is addressing?
Supporting learning goal	What is the scientific explanation that you expect students to provide in response to the "big idea" question? What evidence and/or examples will you consider to be acceptable in response to this question?
Step 2: Finding Out What Students Know	
Assessment purpose	How will students respond to the big idea question at this point in the unit? How do they support their answer with evidence and examples learned in class?
Placement in unit	How far into the unit will you wait before asking students to respond to the "big idea" question for the first time? How often will you revisit the question?
Assessment activity	Will students work individually or in a small group? If students are working in a small group, should they collect all the different answers that they have within the group or come to a consensus? Will there be a whole-class conversation in which students share and defend their ideas?
Data to be collected about student learning	How will you categorize students' different responses? Will you read through all of their individual responses, or will you listen to what they present to the whole class?
Step 3: Anticipating Feedback	
Probable student alternative conceptions	What common prior ideas and misunderstandings do you expect students to express in response to the question? What elements of the question do you anticipate students will not yet understand? What prior experiences or everyday examples from outside of class do you expect them to share?
Feedback ideas	How can you help students focus on the evidence and examples studied in class to support their conclusions? How can you help them to explain their prior ideas through the lens of the acceptable scientific explanation?

HOW CAN I ENACT BIG IDEA QUESTIONS IN MY CLASSROOM?

Since the purpose of a big idea question is to find out what individual students know, it's best if all students respond to the question individually. Be sure to give students plenty of time in your class to give their responses because many are likely to get frustrated at first when a short answer does not come immediately to mind. Take note of who is not writing and encourage these students to think broadly about the question and how they might apply what they know to answer it.

After students have answered the questions individually, you have a number of different options in terms of how to proceed. Since they are open-ended by nature, big idea questions work well as think-pair-share activities, so that students can first think and write their own responses and then pair with someone sitting near them to discuss and preprocess their answer before sharing with the class. This approach works well early in a unit where the purpose is just to find out what students know. Later in a unit, you might also ask students to develop a consensus response in pairs or in small groups so that students are forced to look at different responses and decide which fits the question best. As previously mentioned, if you use science notebooks with your class, you could also use the big idea question as a journaling activity, asking students to return to the question multiple times throughout unit Different colors of pen can help you track how students' ideas changed over time.

If you do hold a discussion or ask students to speak in groups, it is still important to take a look at individual student responses after class. Research has shown that the students who speak after a big idea question are more likely to give the responses that are correct, whereas students who are less sure of their answers and have incorrect or incomplete responses may not share their answers with a larger group (Furtak & Ruiz-Primo, 2008). This means that while having students speaking in class may serve the purpose of students hearing each other's responses, the time spent after class reading through students' responses helps to give you a more realistic profile of what the students in your class know, which can then serve as a basis for giving feedback to those students who need it.

Figure 5.1 summarizes these different steps in enacting big idea questions as formative assessments. First, develop a big idea question based on the content standard you'll be addressing, pose that question to the class, and have students respond individually. Then engage students in some kind of activity in which they share their ideas with partners, small groups, and/or the whole class. Afterward, you should read through all student responses. Once you have compared your class's responses to your learning goals, plan instruction accordingly and provide feedback to the whole class and individuals as necessary.

Figure 5.1 Sequence for Enacting Big Ideas Formative Assessments

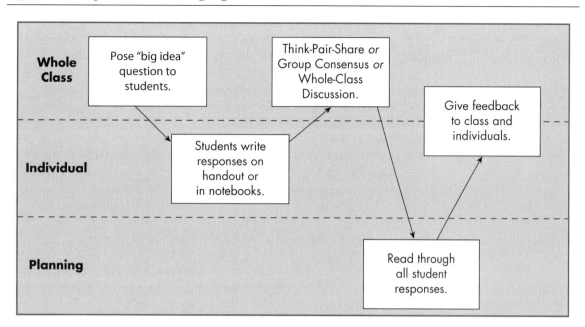

BIG IDEA QUESTION EXAMPLE 5.1: SCIENTIFIC QUESTIONS

Step 1: Setting Learning Goals	
Science content	The National Science Education Standards 6–8 for understanding science as inquiry states that students should be able to engage in full and in partial inquiries, starting with identifying questions that can be answered through scientific investigations.
Supporting learning goal	The students will come to know that a good scientific question is specific, based on observable phenomena, includes scientific ideas and concepts and, in some cases, involves a statement of what is being tested and what is being controlled. The students will be able to write and critique scientific questions based on these criteria.
Step 2: Finding Out What Students Know	
Assessment purpose	In order to assess a key part of designing a scientific investigation, students are asked to explain what constitutes a good scientific question.

(Continued)

(Continued)

Placement in unit	The short-answer question is being given to students toward the beginning of a unit titled "What kind of a scientist am I?" The unit is placed at the end of the school year and is intended to help students reflect on and review all they have learned about the process of science through the course of the school year.
Assessment activity	Students will respond to the question individually before the teacher collects the students' responses to read later. Then, the teacher will hold a brief discussion with students to hear what they know about the qualities of a good scientific question.
Data to be collected about student learning	The teacher will listen to ideas presented by individual students to the whole class, but will base her feedback on information she gets from reading through students' responses after class.
Step 3: Anticipating Feedback	
Probable student alternative conceptions	While students may not have actual alternative conceptions about scientific questions, it is very likely that they will not focus on the same criteria that scientists might use. Students are likely to remember that their questions are supposed to be specific and clear but may not remember that they need to be testable and focus upon control and experimental variables.
Feedback ideas	If the majority of the class does not articulate all the features of scientifically oriented questions in their responses, the teacher may decide to explicitly talk about them in the next class. An activity in which students evaluate a number of different scientific questions will help them apply these features, and then asking students to revise poorly worded questions will help them to put these features to use.

Science Content Standard is from National Research Council. (1996). *National Science Education Standards.* Washington, DC: National Academies Press.

BIG IDEA QUESTION

Name: _____

Date: _____

Please answer the following question. Write as much information as you need to explain your answer. Use evidence and examples to support your explanation.

How do you write a good scientific question?

Formative Assessment in Action: Big Idea Questions

Ms. Holmes was nearing the end of the school year and wanted to reflect with her students on one of the overarching learning goals that had framed her science class for that school year: What kind of scientist am I? She worked to help students view themselves as scientists and to think about the different kinds of skills they had developed through the year. Students had been asked to apply what they had learned to develop their own scientific investigations during their current unit, so Ms. Holmes decided to frame a question to her students that homed in on a framing question for that unit: the characteristics of a scientific question. She prepared a simple handout for her students for the question, "How do you write a good scientific question?"

During class on the day she gave the formative assessment, Ms. Holmes began by reminding her students about the work they had done all year.

"We've done a bit of work on this topic during the year," she began. "If you remember, we had a discussion about what makes a good scientific question. For example, when we were investigating enzymes earlier in the year, we asked, 'What makes pineapple jelly set?'"

After waiting a moment to check students' expressions for signs of remembering this investigation, Ms. Holmes also reminded them about investigations from earlier in the year that they had done with creating and using identification keys, as well as investigating the structure and properties of snow.

Ms. Holmes then said, "I'm going to hand out a sheet to you now; it's very short, and the question is very clear. I'd like you to answer this question to the best of your abilities, and I am very interested in what *you* are thinking about it."

Ms. Holmes walked around the room, giving the formative assessments to students individually. After a pause of a minute during which students filled in their name and the date, there was a flurry of activity as a few students were unsure as to how to get started. Several pulled out their science notebooks, flipping through furiously in search of an answer to the question. Ms. Holmes simply smiled, saying, "Your notebook won't help you; it's what's up here," as she tapped the top of her head. "But you can use it to refresh your memory if you like."

As the students got down to work, several called her over, asking for clarification. Ms. Holmes provided several hints:

- "Think about what would make a question *good.*"
- "What do you think?"
- "What experiences have you had?"
- "It's not a memory test; it's based on what *you* think."

While half of the class was finished after about 15 minutes of writing, Ms. Holmes gave the class another five minutes so that all students had a chance to write something down. When the five minutes were over, she walked around the room and collected all of the students' papers.

While Ms. Holmes primarily wanted to read through students' responses, she had about five minutes left in class and decided to use it to get a preview of what some of her students had written. She asked the class, "Now, I would like a little feedback from you. Who would like to share with us what they had for that answer? Remember, there's no right or wrong answer; this is about your opinion. Yes, Ahmed?"

"To do a good scientific question, you have to have a question that is specific and has information about what you want to do," said Ahmed, glancing at his paper. "And it needs to be easy to understand."

"Ah, so if it's general, it's not as good?"

"No, so if you have like, 'What does X do?' you need to make it more specific."

"Thanks, Ahmed," said Ms. Holmes, smiling as she scanned the classroom, "Lisa, what have you got?"

Lisa replied, "A good scientific question is a question that you can investigate, so something you want to know and something you can test."

Ms. Holmes furrowed her brow and asked, **"**When you say something that can be tested, what do you mean?"

"Like, through an experiment."

With a slight nod, Ms. Holmes turned to the rest of the class, saying, "What other skills do we have in science that are special to science? What makes carrying out a good scientific experiment different from other skills?" Several male students responded in tandem without raising their hands.

"Lighting a Bunsen burner?" "Learning to control variables."

Ms. Holmes said, "Yeah, controlling variables, what else?"

Sasha added, "Looking at the details."

"Yes, looking at the details, like observation skills. Okay," said Ms. Holmes as the bell rang, signaling the end of class. Ms. Holmes thanked the students for their participation and let them know she would read their responses before the next class.

When Ms. Holmes looked at the responses later, she saw that one was completely blank, and a few more students had written only a sentence or two in the time they have been provided, but she noted who those students were, remembering that even blank responses are information about what students do *not* know.

Since the students had a lot of time to write, many of them wrote a paragraph or more about what they thought made a good scientific question. At first glance, Ms. Holmes found some of the questions hard to interpret. Many students had written several different ideas down. However, after reading through the work of all her students, Ms. Holmes noticed several themes that emerged.

Many of the student responses focused on the importance of clarity, like the student in the response shown in Figure 5.2.

Figure 5.2 Big Ideas: Student Response 1

What makes a good scientific question?

I think a scientific question is a good question when you don't know the answer already. A very good question is a research question (something you can research about). It needs to be direct but not long and it does not have to sound difficult. It can be easy to understand.

A smaller set of students also thought that good questions needed to have scientific words in them. Only a small number of the students were able to put into words what Ms. Holmes had been looking for—that scientific questions should be testable, as shown in Figure 5.3.

(Continued)

(Continued)

Figure 5.3 Big Ideas: Student Response 2

> *What makes a good scientific question?*
>
> A good scientific question is when you can answer it with a experiment.
> Or when you can make a hipothosies to it- you should cnow how to prove it.
> So how to make an experiment to prove it.

When she compared the selection of responses she got in class along with her brief read-through of the students' responses, Ms. Holmes realized that while students seemed to understand that their scientific questions needed to be very clearly stated, they still needed to focus on the idea that scientific questions are also testable. The next day, Ms. Holmes talked about these results in general at the beginning of class to let students know that while scientific questions indeed need to be clearly written, she felt there was still something missing from many of their responses. In the remaining investigations left in the school year, she also hoped to more explicitly talk about the importance of questions being testable and different types of variables. In addition, she made plans to focus on the criteria for scientific questions during the next school year.

BIG IDEA QUESTION EXAMPLE 5.2: WORK AND ENERGY

Step 1: Setting Learning Goals	
Science content	The National Science Education Standards' Physical Science Content Standard B states that all students should develop an understanding of conservation of energy. In Grades 9–12, students should understand that "All energy can be considered to be either kinetic energy, which is the energy of motion; potential energy, which depends on relative position; or energy contained by a field, such as electromagnetic waves."
Supporting learning goal	The students will be able to qualitatively relate how a quantity of stored energy is present in a gallon of gas and talk about how that is transferred to kinetic energy of the motion of the center of mass of the car, the motion of all of the parts of the car,

	and the loss of useful energy to friction and drag. Then, students should find a direct relationship between the amount and rate of energy delivery to a useful function, and the loss to nonuseful channels, and estimate what all of this costs.
Step 2: Finding Out What Students Know	
Assessment purpose	Since this standard is about connecting seemingly disparate systems, the content can be framed in terms of an everyday event that students would be able to explain after learning about the concepts of stored energy in fuel, kinetic energy of a car, and the loss of useful energy to friction and drag. There is a direct relationship between the amount and rate of energy delivery to a useful function, the loss to nonuseful channels, and what all of this costs. This interpretation of the standard leads to the big idea question, "Why does it cost so much to drive a car?"
Placement in unit	This question can be used three times within a unit on work and energy; once as a preassessment to see what students know at the beginning of the unit, one midunit to see how they are starting to apply what they learned, and at the end to see if they can bring together everything they know to answer the question.
Assessment activity	Students should respond to the question individually, and then—depending on the placement of the assessment in the unit—could share their ideas with the class or speak together in a group to come to a consensus about one answer. Students will evaluate the quality of different responses and develop more refined answers to help them move toward the learning goal.
Data to be collected about student learning	Individual student responses to the big idea question.
Step 3: Anticipating Feedback	
Probable student alternative conceptions	Students will confuse the concept of average speed with instantaneous speed or just the speed of an object.
Feedback ideas	Get the student to appreciate that the instantaneous speed is the thing that a car's speedometer measures. (It's a well-defined quantity at any instant.) On the other hand, average speed has to do with the entire trip that takes place over an extended time period. It would be the number you would get by dividing the overall distance traveled by the overall time that the trip took.

Science Content Standard is from National Research Council. (1996). *National Science Education Standards*, p. 180. Washington, DC: National Academies Press.

BIG IDEA QUESTION

Name: _____

Date: _____

We're trying to develop an answer to the following question while we're studying work and energy. When you give your answer, be sure to draw upon what you've learned in class.

Why does it cost so much to drive a car?

Concept Maps

WHAT IS A CONCEPT MAP?

Flip open an average science textbook from your school, choose an arbitrary chapter, and count the words that are marked in **bold**—these "key terms" add up amazingly quickly and illustrate the incredible size of the new vocabulary we expect students to learn in science. Most scientists would agree that not every student on the street needs to be able to explain all of the steps in cellular respiration, but they would probably say that students should know what happens when they breathe and understand that the oxygen that they breathe in is used by their cells to release energy contained in their food. Furthermore, there is a set of scientific terms—*cell, lung, carbon dioxide,* for example—that are considered important for all citizens in a scientific society to know (American Association for the Advancement of Science, 1990). To participate in the process of science, both as students and as future citizens, students need to learn to speak and truly understand the language of science. It's common in traditional science education to give students a list of vocabulary words and ask them to write their definitions or to use those words in sentences. However, just knowing what a word means is not enough; research shows that if students do not connect new concepts to older ones, they will not remember them because they do not know how they relate to each other. In order to be able to answer the important *why* and *how* questions of science, students need to understand how important concepts are connected together in networks or schema (Li, Ruiz-Primo, & Shavelson, 2006).

Concept maps are one approach to finding out how students are—or are not—able to relate different terms to each other. Concept maps are graphical representations of the relationships among concepts (Vanides, Yin, Tomita, & Ruiz-Primo, 2005). The purpose of a concept map is to get at students' understanding not only of the important ideas, terms, and concepts but also how concepts are related to each other. Students making concept maps connect words with one-way arrows labeled with linking phrases so that the relationship between the two terms can be read as a sentence.

Take, for example, a concept map about the rock cycle. Students are provided with a list of words—we'll call them *concept terms*—including magma, metamorphic rocks, and igneous rocks. The term *magma* can be connected to the term *igneous rocks* with the linking phrase *hardens and cools to form*, making the sentence, "Magma hardens and cools to form igneous rocks." Then, magma can also be connected to metamorphic rocks with the phrase, "melts to form." Metamorphic and igneous rocks can be connected to each other to form the sentence, "Igneous rocks under heat and pressure become metamorphic rocks." These connections begin to form a network of concept terms and linking phrases as shown in Figure 6.1.

By asking your students to make a map like this, you are going beyond just asking for definitions, which are not often connected to each other.

Figure 6.1   Example of a Concept Map for the Rock Cycle

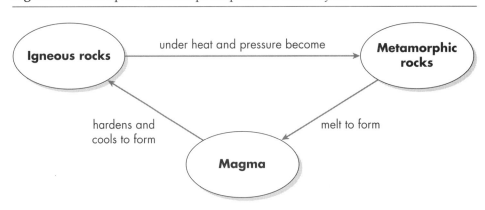

According to Vanides et al. (2005), concept maps display how students are organizing and connecting information, giving your students opportunities to do the following (p. 28):

1. Think about the connections between the science terms being learned.

2. Organize their thoughts and visualize the relationships between key concepts in a systematic way.

3. Reflect on their understanding.

In addition to these opportunities, concept maps also give you the chance to look at how well your students are building a network of knowledge around key concepts they should learn. True experts in a content area are able to make concept maps with many integrated connections between concept terms (Chi, Glaser, & Far, 1988), so you can gauge your students' learning progress by looking at the quality and quantity of their connections and the way those connections are organized.

WHEN SHOULD I USE CONCEPT MAPS IN MY UNIT?

Concept maps are wonderfully flexible as formative assessments since they can be used anywhere in a unit and can even be used multiple times to track students' developing understanding. Use them at the beginning of a unit to preassess what students know and then give students time to revise or redraw the same concept map later to see which concept terms students are integrating into their knowledge and which concept terms they still need to learn. You can also look for alternative conceptions in students' incorrect connections between concept terms or for unclear links between terms, which reveal that students haven't quite understood how those terms are related. In this way, concept maps can help you to keep a running record of how your students are improving through a unit.

Use concept maps as formative assessments at the points in a unit where students really need to integrate particular concepts before moving forward—for example, after completing a supporting learning goal that is an essential part of the unit. Vanides et al. (2005) suggest that concept maps can be especially useful in helping teachers to understand students' ideas after inquiry-based investigations since they call students' attention to the important concepts that underlie the activity they just completed.

HOW CAN I DEVELOP MY OWN CONCEPT MAPS?

When deciding which terms should go into your concept map, start by looking at the goals you have developed for your curriculum unit and identify the most essential concepts that you want students to come to know. You can use the planning sheet from the beginning chapters to help you in this process; a version of that planning sheet is shown here with suggestions for what to think about at each step (Table 6.1).

Once you've come up with your list of concept terms, make your own map with them, keeping concept terms that can be integrated into a network and discarding those that are difficult to connect, until you have about six to eight terms and no more than 10 or 12. If you have fewer than six terms, it will be more difficult for students to make multiple, network-like connections between them. If you have more, the concept map will get quite complicated very quickly and will be difficult to interpret.

Then insert these terms into the format for concept maps included at the end of this chapter. Rich Shavelson and the Stanford Education Assessment Laboratory have developed this format through many years of research, and I'll explain it more in the next section.

Table 6.1   Planning Process for Concept Map Formative Assessments

Step 1: Setting Learning Goals	
Science content	What standard will you be addressing with the formative assessment?
Supporting learning goal	What are the important concepts that students will come to know?
Step 2: Finding Out What Students Know	
Assessment purpose	Why do students need to be able to relate these particular terms? What propositions between terms do you want them to be able to make?
Placement in unit	Will students know all of the concept terms when they work on the map or only some? Will students complete the concept map only once or multiple times as they progress through the unit?
Assessment activity	Will students work on their maps individually or also in small groups? Will you hold a discussion about connecting key concept terms after they have worked on their own?
Data to be collected about student learning	Will you look at individual maps or group maps? What kinds of conversations will you be looking for as students are working in groups?
Step 3: Anticipating Feedback	
Probable student alternative conceptions	Which concept terms do you expect students will have more trouble connecting with the others? What are the common misunderstandings, prior beliefs, or misconceptions that might be exposed in students' propositions?
Feedback ideas	How can you help students to relate *orphan* concept terms with ones they already understand? How might you help students with incorrect propositions make more accurate connections?

HOW CAN I ENACT CONCEPT MAPS IN MY CLASSROOM?

The way that you enact a concept map in your classroom is very closely tied to the format you're using. I suggest you use the template developed by the Stanford Education Assessment Laboratory, as I described above. There are two different versions of this template at the end of the chapter. It has four pages:

1. A cover page with an example map and rules for making a concept map
2. A practice concept map page for the water cycle
3. A rough draft of the concept map with a list of terms
4. A final draft page

To save paper, you may choose to have students paste a copy of the first page in their science notebooks so they can refer to it each time they make a concept map. You may also consider providing students with enough small sticky notes so that they can write each concept term on a note and then move them around as they construct the rough draft of the map.

The first time that you enact a concept map in your classroom, be sure to leave extra time to teach your students about the rules for making the map. Start by going through the different pages with your students in four steps, here summarized from Vanides et al. (2005).

Step 1: Teach Students to Make Maps

It is possible students may have made concept maps in other classes, but they may not use the same procedure for doing so (e.g., it's common to make concept maps with no linking phrases). Thus, it's important to explicitly go through the steps of making a concept maps with your students the first one or two times.

Read through the rules with your students on the first page of the concept map and use the "Rose is a type of flower" map on the right of that page to illustrate your points. Then, you may create the sample practice map for the water cycle on page two by writing it on the board and asking students to provide connections between the phrases until it seems that they understand the procedure (page 2). Use this as an opportunity to discuss quality of links, encouraging students to make the most specific and scientific links between concept terms that they can.

Step 2: Make Individual Maps

On pages 3 and 4, have students make maps individually. To promote students' thinking about the interrelationships between concept terms, have students make the maps individually first. If they work as a class first, it takes a lot of class time and is not necessarily engaging for all students. Give students plenty of time to create a rough draft of their map and time to make a final version on the next page, which is often more complex than the original. As students work, go around the room and check that students are applying the rules for concept maps (e.g., using connecting phrases and not crossing lines between terms).

Step 3: Students Review Maps in Groups

In small groups, have students review their maps. This may be done as a pair, where students look for similarities and differences in their maps and talk about them. In this way, you're engaging students in the social process of science, an important aspect of science teaching and learning (National Research Council, 2001). You may allow students to revisit their maps at this point, although you may want them to do it in a different color of pencil so you know the difference between what they did individually and what they did in a group.

Step 4: Whole-Class Discussion

After students discuss their maps in small groups, you may go around the room and ask each group to share one or two important links on their concept maps, explaining why they chose to connect those terms in that way. If you like, write these connections on the board to create a whole-class map, asking students to decide which connections are the best. Try to focus students on what you think are the key connections. Step 5 is necessary only if you feel, after students have worked in groups, that you need to reinforce some of the concepts as a whole class—in effect, to begin to give feedback about the quality of different important links. These steps are summarized in Figure 6.2.

Making Sense of Concept Maps

Once you have collected the maps, it's time to make sense of them for your instruction in order to plan your next lessons and to find out how well students are doing at meeting learning goals. If you're using concept maps as formative assessments, you should not use a formal system for

Figure 6.2 Sequence for Enacting Concept Map Formative Assessments

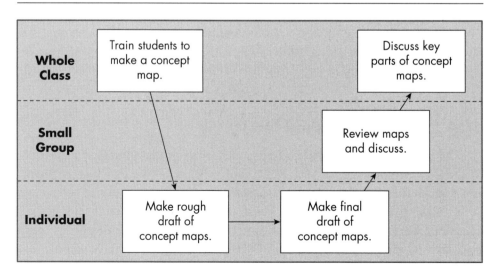

evaluating them and should not assign grades to them. Remember, grading formative assessments defeats their purpose of informing teaching and learning in a low-stakes environment. Vanides et al. (2005) suggest three different ways of qualitatively looking at the maps to find out what your students know and providing feedback to improve student learning.

Complexity

This is probably the easiest way to look at the map, trying to see if it is a complex network or more linear or circular, or looks like a wheel (hub concept in the middle attached to spokes). These kinds of patterns are shown in Figures 6.3, 6.4, and 6.5.

Importance of Links

Based on where you are in the unit, you probably have a good idea of what the most important links between concepts are in your map. Write two or three of these down and use them as an informal rubric as you observe students working, looking for these important links in each student's map. If a student is missing these key connections, then you know this student will need some feedback or more focused instruction on these concepts. Then, each time you use the concept map, revise and add to your list of important links that you'd like students to be able to make.

Quality of Links

Think about which links are better than others—certainly, there are connections between concepts that are simply incorrect, but you may go

Figure 6.3 Linear Concept Map Pattern

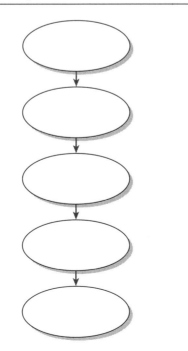

Figure 6.4 Hub Concept Map Pattern

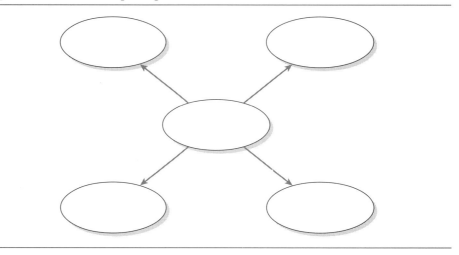

Figure 6.5 Network Concept Map Pattern

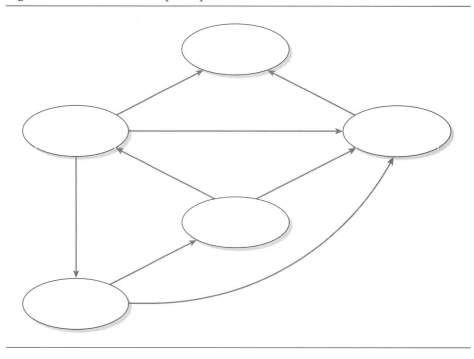

further in specifying degrees of quality. Vanides et al. (2005) suggest using three levels of scoring—incorrect, partially correct and/or scientifically weak, and scientifically correct. Marking these different levels with different colors of pen can be time consuming but can also help you and your students home in on areas to be improved.

As you plan your own concept map formative assessments, use the examples at the end of this chapter as a guide, as well as Planning Sheet E in the Resources.

CONCEPT MAP EXAMPLE 6.1: POLLUTANTS IN THE ATMOSPHERE

Step 1: Setting Learning Goals	
Science content	The National Science Education Standards for Science in Personal and Social Perspectives in Grades 9–12 Earth and Space Science Content Standard state that students should develop understanding of environmental quality. Students should come to understand that humans are changing the natural process of maintaining the atmosphere and that the changes may be detrimental to humans. In addition, the Physical Science Standards state that students should understand the reactions contributing to the presence of ozone and greenhouse gases in the atmosphere and the burning and processing of fossil fuels.
Supporting learning goal	Students will be able to relate different pollutants to their sources and consequences in the atmosphere.
Step 2: Finding Out What Students Know	
Assessment purpose	Students should understand that methane, sulfur dioxide, and carbon monoxide are all released into the atmosphere as pollutants created by the production or burning of fossil fuels. They should also know that methane and carbon dioxide are greenhouse gases and thus contribute to global warming, whereas sulfur dioxide can dissolve in water to produce acid rain.
Placement in unit	Students are partway through a unit on air and air pollution. The concept maps will serve as a check to see how well students are able to connect the terms together.
Assessment activity	The teacher will use the "Concept Map Instructions" page to explain the procedure for making concept maps with students. The students will then complete the concept map individually, using sticky notes to arrange concept terms between a draft and final map. Then they will work in small groups to construct a group map, having conversations about where concept terms should go and how they should be linked.
Data to be collected about student learning	The teacher will circulate to groups, listening in and asking questions.
Step 3: Anticipating Feedback	
Probable student alternative conceptions	Students may think that all chemicals released into the atmosphere have the potential to produce acid rain. Students may not know that all three gases in the concept map are related in some way to fossil fuels. Students may link acid rain to greenhouse gases or global warming.
Feedback ideas	Focus on talking about the mechanism behind global warming and how greenhouse gases contribute to it. Explore with students the composition of fossil fuels and how different pollutants are formed during their production or consumption. Talk about the differences between the mechanisms leading to acid rain and global warming.

Science Content Standard is from National Research Council. (1996). *National Science Education Standards.* Washington, DC: National Academies Press.

CONCEPT MAP INSTRUCTIONS

Name: _____

Date: _____

A concept map is a drawing that represents your thinking about a topic. It includes the following:

- Concept terms (in circles or on sticky notes)
- One-way arrows that relate two concept terms
- Linking words or phrases that label the arrows and describe the relationship between a pair of concept terms

Rules for Constructing a Concept Map

- Concept terms appear only once on the map
- The map can be organized any way you want
- Use only the concept terms that are provided
- Use only one labeled arrow between two concepts
- You can link a concept term to more than one other concept but use separately labeled arrows
- You can only draw arrows between concepts, not to another arrow

An example of a concept map is shown here.

Concept Terms

Rose	Florist
Flower	Feeling
Fragrance	Love

Fragrance

can have a

has a

Flower

is a type of

can be bought at the

can be purchased at a

Florist ← Rose

can be expressed by a

is a symbol of

Feeling ← is a type of ← Love

Source: Stanford Education Assessment Laboratory. (2003). *Teacher's Guide to the Reflective Lessons.* Unpublished manuscript.

POLLUTION IN THE ATMOSPHERE CONCEPT MAP

Name: _____

Date: _____

Step 1: Draw a Concept Map

Draw a concept map using the concept terms listed in the box, following the rules for creating a concept map. Start by making a rough draft on the next page. If you like, you can write each of the concept terms on sticky notes so that you can move them around as you work.

You may use any linking phrase you choose to best describe the relationship between pairs of concept terms.

Concept Terms

- Methane (CH_4)
- Global Warming
- Atmosphere
- Acid Rain

- Greenhouse Gas
- Carbon Monoxide (CO)
- Sulfur Dioxide (SO_2)
- Fossil Fuels

Step 2: Check Your Work

When you are finished, make sure that you have checked the following:

All the concept terms appear only once on your map.

All the linking lines are labeled with a linking phrase.

Your map makes sense when you read it. (See the example map: "Rose is a type of flower.")

Step 3: Redraw Your Concept Map

When you are done checking your map, redraw the final version so someone else can read it.

Source: Stanford Education Assessment Laboratory. (2003). *Teacher's Guide to the Reflective Lessons.* Unpublished manuscript.

POLLUTION IN THE ATMOSPHERE
CONCEPT MAP, ROUGH DRAFT

Name: _____

Date: _____

Concept Terms

- Methane (CH_4)
- Global Warming
- Atmosphere
- Acid Rain

- Greenhouse Gas
- Carbon Monoxide (CO)
- Sulfur Dioxide (SO_2)
- Fossil Fuels

POLLUTION IN THE ATMOSPHERE CONCEPT MAP, FINAL DRAFT

Name: _____

Date: _____

Concept Terms

- Methane (CH_4)
- Global Warming
- Atmosphere
- Acid Rain

- Greenhouse Gas
- Carbon Monoxide (CO)
- Sulfur Dioxide (SO_2)
- Fossil Fuels

Formative Assessment in Action: Pollution in the Atmosphere Concept Map

Ms. Holmes and her ninth-grade chemistry class were in the middle of a unit about the atmosphere, and she wanted to check their understanding of how different pollutants were released into the air.

Looking back at her unit, Ms. Holmes was able to identify a number of different environmental pollutants that were related in some way and wanted to explore the kinds of connections her students were (or were not) able to make between them. She took a set of the concepts, wrote them onto sticky notes, and made a map herself. She found a few terms that did not have straightforward relationships to the others, so she replaced them with other terms. Eventually, she was able to get a set of concepts that represented the learning goals or big ideas she was teaching and that could be connected with each other in meaningful ways.

Using the template for formative assessments developed by the Stanford Education Assessment Laboratory (SEAL) shown in the previous pages, Ms. Holmes identified what she felt were the most important terms she wanted students to know and wrote those into the "Concept Terms" box.

Ms. Holmes's students had never made a concept map before, so she took a few minutes to explain concept maps at the beginning of class on the day she did her formative assessment.

"We can use a concept map to link up key concept terms from the last couple of lessons," she said. "As you remember, we've been speaking about the atmosphere around us and sources of global warming. We've also spoken about acid rain and how that happens. Now, I'd like to know how well you understand how all those different terms we've been throwing around are connected to each other.

"Put down your own ideas, not those of others. I am interested in finding out what you know about how these concepts are connected."

Then Ms. Holmes walked around the room, passing out the concept maps and making sure each student had enough sticky notes. She asked students to write the concepts on the sticky notes, encouraging them to move the sticky notes around as they drew and modified their maps. She also asked students to be sure to use pencil since, when she made the map, she found that she made a lot of changes that required a lot of erasing.

Students got to work but initially had a lot of questions. Ms. Holmes noticed right away that before students could even begin making connections between the concept terms, many of them needed to review what each term meant. They asked questions about the definition of particular words—greenhouse gas and sulfur dioxide. Ms. Holmes encouraged these students to look back through their notebooks, making a mental note of which students were struggling.

One student was not even sure how to begin, so Ms. Holmes gave her some process-related feedback to help her get started. "Try by starting with two words that you know are related, then think of a phrase that would connect those words to make a short sentence. So start by thinking about how just two words or concepts are related and then take one of those words and connect it to another and then just keep going. Does that make sense?" The student nodded and got to work.

As the class period went on, students began making connections between concept terms on their maps, and Ms. Holmes wandered around the classroom, reminding students of the rules for making concept maps when necessary. As she circulated between desks, several students stopped her to ask, "Is it right?" while pointing at a connection between concept terms. Each time, Ms. Holmes would refocus students on developing a link between concept terms that they knew rather than worrying as much about getting a right answer.

When most of the students had completed a rough draft of their own maps, she encouraged them to begin working with the person sitting beside them to refine and improve their maps. Students turned to each other and began chatting eagerly, looking over each other's maps and talking about the connections they had made. Several of the students erased some of the linking phrases they had written down and replaced them with better ones after talking to their classmates.

At the end of the period, Ms. Holmes thanked the students for their efforts and collected the concept maps. One of the students—the same one who earlier had not known where to start—had struggled to make any connections at all (Figure 6.6).

Figure 6.6   Concept Map: Student Response 1

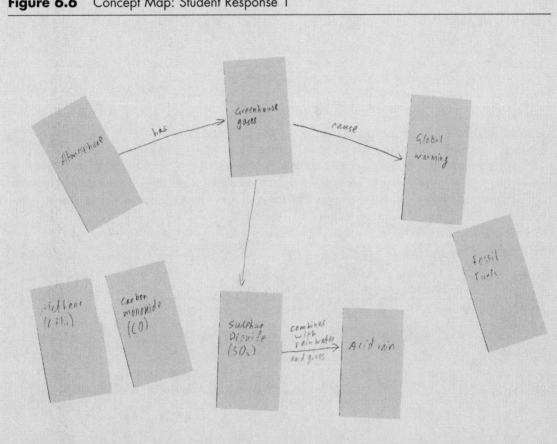

However, the three connections she had made were accurate, and one in particular was very specific: sulfur dioxide—combines with rainwater—acid rain. Ms. Holmes wrote "to form" before acid rain to help the student see that the connection could be further clarified. Then she wrote a comment to the student stating she had a good start on her concept map, but needed to develop her connections to be more specific, like the connection she had made between sulfur dioxide and acid rain.

On the other maps created by students, Ms. Holmes found a network of connections, but the maps varied in terms of the quality of the connections students had made. Many students used linking phrases such as *harms the, caused by,* and *found in* almost exclusively (Figures 6.7 and 6.8).

(Continued)

(Continued)

Figure 6.7   Concept Map: Student Response 2

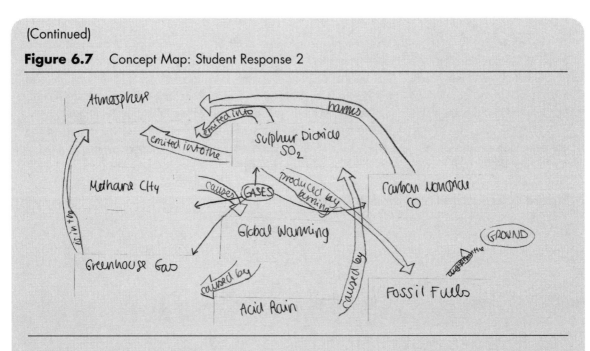

On these maps, Ms. Holmes circled the linking phrases that contained more details about how the two concept terms were linked and then asked students to think about how the other connections could be made more specific. On some of these maps, Ms. Holmes noticed unclear connections, such as "Atmosphere prevents global warming," and would mark them with statements such as, "Are you sure about this?" and "Try this one again and think about how these two things are really related."

Figure 6.8   Concept Map: Student Response 3

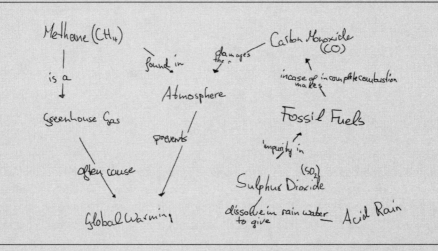

Overall, Ms. Holmes felt that the assessment was productive in helping her distinguish those students who had learned enough about the concepts to make specific and clear connections from those who made general connections between concept terms, as well as those students who could make only a few or inaccurate connections. To help her students improve their work, Ms. Holmes planned the next day to put her students into small groups and to have them construct a map as a group. She planned to have her students focus on the quality of connections between concept terms, and then share their concept maps as a class. As a follow-up activity, Ms. Holmes found an article for her students to read about atmospheric pollutants to help them think about real-world examples of these concept terms.

CONCEPT MAP EXAMPLE 6.2: ELECTRICITY

Step 1: Setting Learning Goals	
Science content	The National Science Education Standards for Physical Science for Grades 9–12 state that students should come to understand conservation of energy and how energy and matter interact. A powerful way to address these objectives is through the study of batteries and light bulbs. In addition to directly concentrating on electromotive force, current, and resistance, these lessons show how energy is transferred through electricity and energy is conserved.
Supporting learning goal	Students will learn how a current behaves in series and parallel circuits and will distinguish between the concepts of electromotive force, current, and resistance.
Step 2: Finding Out What Students Know	
Assessment purpose	Students will recognize that current flows from a battery in inverse proportion to the total resistance of the connected circuit consisting of a simple network of bulbs (Ohm's law). They will be able to predict the effect of both series and parallel combinations of bulbs and will be able to reduce the network to a single effective load on the battery. In demonstrating this understanding, they will use the concept of energy conservation, as represented by Kirchhoff's loop rule.
Placement in unit	Students will already have learned that current must flow through a complete circuit and that current is not used up in a bulb. They will know that the brightness of a bulb is related to the amount of current flowing through the bulb and will have had experience with simple electrical circuits consisting of a battery and a single bulb.
Assessment activity	Students will first complete the concept map individually, using sticky notes to arrange concept terms between a draft and final map. Then they will work in small groups to construct a group map, having conversations about where concept terms should go and how they should be linked.
Data to be collected about student learning	The teacher will circulate to groups, listening in and asking questions.
Step 3: Anticipating Feedback	
Probable student alternative conceptions	Students may think that current and voltage are the same.
Feedback ideas	Try to get the students to make the connections between what goes on in a circuit and how water flows through a pipe or hose. The voltage in a wire is like the pressure in a pipe, while the current in the wire is like the water that's flowing through the pipe.

Science Content Standard is from National Research Council. (1996). *National Science Education Standards.* Washington, DC: National Academies Press.

CONCEPT MAP INSTRUCTIONS

Name: _____

Date: _____

A concept map is a drawing that represents your thinking about a topic. It includes the following:

- Concept terms (in circles or on sticky notes)
- One-way arrows that relate two concept terms
- Linking words or phrases that label the arrows and describe the relationship between a pair of concept terms

Rules for Constructing a Concept Map

- Concept terms appear only once on the map
- The map can be organized any way you want
- Use only the concept terms that are provided
- Use only one labeled arrow between two concepts
- You can link a concept term to more than one other concept but use separate labeled arrows
- You can draw arrows only between concepts, not to another arrow

An example of a concept map is shown here.

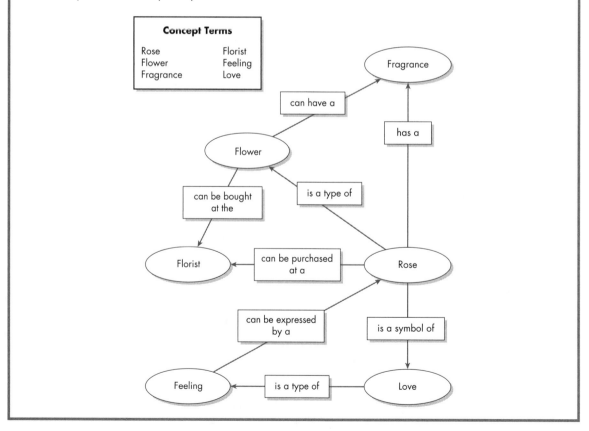

Source: Stanford Education Assessment Laboratory. (2003). *Teacher's Guide to the Reflective Lessons.* Unpublished manuscript.

ELECTRICITY CONCEPT MAP

Name: _____

Date: _____

Step 1: Draw a Concept Map

Draw a concept map using the concept terms listed in the box to your right, following the rules for creating a concept map. Start by making a rough draft on the next page. If you like, you can write each of the concept terms on sticky notes so that you can move them around as you work.

You may use any linking phrase you choose to best describe the relationship between pairs of concept terms.

Concept Terms

- Electromotive Force
- Voltage Drop
- Electric Current
- Heat

- Resistance of Material
- Power Transformation
- Light

Step 2: Check Your Work

When you are finished, make sure that you have checked the following:

All the concept terms appear only once on your map.

All the linking lines are labeled with a linking phrase.

Your map makes sense when you read it. (See the example map, "Rose is a type of flower.")

Step 3: Redraw Your Concept Map

When you are done checking your map, redraw the final version so someone else can read it.

Source: Stanford Education Assessment Laboratory. (2003). *Teacher's Guide to the Reflective Lessons.* Unpublished manuscript.

ELECTRICITY CONCEPT MAP, ROUGH DRAFT

Name: _____

Date: _____

Concept Terms

- Electromotive Force
- Voltage Drop
- Electric Current
- Heat

- Resistance of Material
- Power Transformation
- Light

ELECTRICITY CONCEPT MAP, FINAL DRAFT

Name: _____

Date: _____

Concept Terms

- Electromotive Force
- Voltage Drop
- Electric Current
- Heat

- Resistance of Material
- Power Transformation
- Light

7

Predict-Observe-Explain (POE) Assessments

WHAT IS A POE?

Asking students to predict what will happen during an event, observe that event take place, and explain the accuracy or inaccuracy of their own predictions is an effective way to engage students, get them to share their ideas, and promote argumentation (White & Gunstone, 1992). Events that have unexpected outcomes—what are sometimes called "discrepant events"—can have a powerful impact on students, showing them that the ideas on which their predictions are based may not be accurate.

Predict-Observe-Explain (POE) formative assessments have three parts. First, students are presented with an experimental situation and asked to predict what might happen. Second, students observe as the teacher carries out the experiment and record what happened. Third, students are given an opportunity to indicate whether their prediction was correct or incorrect and to explain their reasoning or how their reasoning has changed given their observations.

POEs are essentially redesigned classroom demonstrations. However, unlike demonstrations that simply illustrate a phenomenon, POEs are intended to be discrepant events that force students to move forward in their thinking. One of the most important features of POEs is their excitement factor; by building up the event that will be observed, you can pique students' interest and actually have them demand that you carry out the demonstration so that they can see what happens. Asking them to tell you why they are making a particular prediction gives them a personal stake in the outcome, and when they observe the results, you can expect them to cry out "yes" if they were correct or to gasp in surprise when they learn their reasoning is inaccurate. POEs can help students to realize their present explanations are insufficient and compel them to seek further evidence to refine their understandings.

Like other formative assessments, POEs should never be given a grade. They make a good format for obtaining a general idea of what your students know and providing informational, written feedback if you have the time.

WHEN SHOULD I USE POES IN MY UNIT?

POE assessments are designed to elicit students' explanations about a particular phenomenon that is demonstrated for them by the teacher. Although they can be used to assess students' ability to make a prediction based on concepts they have already learned or situations they have already investigated, they are also well suited to situations and/ or materials with which the students are not yet familiar. In the latter case, the assessment will be less a measure of what students already know and more a measure of how well they can apply what they know to a new situation.

To assess something students already know, administer the POE at the end of an activity or a series of lessons where you want to make sure all students have a particular understanding. POEs also work well as launching pads from the last lesson to new lessons or units. You can use them to present students with an opportunity to see that the knowledge and models they are currently working with do not sufficiently explain a new experimental situation, thus creating a "need to know" that will serve as the rationale for the next lesson or unit.

HOW CAN I DEVELOP MY OWN POES?

Think about good demonstrations that you might already be using as part of your different units that really challenge students' ideas. These kinds of demonstrations are perfect for adapting into POEs. Don't worry about developing a lot of POEs; one or two well placed within a unit can be very powerful learning experiences for the students and can provide valuable information to the teacher about students' understanding.

For example, a biology unit on the cell might feature the teacher displaying an image from a video microscope to show students how saltwater can cause plant cells to lose water and the cell membrane to pull away from the cell wall; this demonstration could be adapted into a POE by explaining the materials first and asking students to predict what will happen when saltwater is placed adjacent to the cells and to provide a scientific explanation for *why*. In a physics class, a teacher could ask students what will happen when a large ball and a small ball are dropped simultaneously; students could then predict the order in which the balls will hit the ground (one before the other or at the same time) and explain why they made that particular prediction.

Regardless of the content that you'll be adapting into a POE, it's important to think out in advance the content being assessed, where you'll place the assessment, and the features of the formative assessment loop that will be relevant to this specific POE, using the planning sheet in Table 7.1.

HOW CAN I ENACT POES IN MY CLASSROOM?

POEs are used productively as a combination of writing and discussion. The kinds of information you get from students during a discussion might not be the same as what students write, as not all students always share their responses with the whole class, and some students may better express their ideas in writing. Research has shown that POEs are more likely to get students to share scientifically accurate ideas aloud, perhaps because students who talk in class feel more confident in their responses. However, students will still write down ideas that might not be as scientifically accurate (Furtak & Ruiz-Primo, 2008). So it's important both to hold a discussion to call students' attention to the ideas that might be accurate and the evidence that supports them, and to read what students have written.

Begin by setting up the equipment for the demonstration and then explain to students what you are going to do. Ask them to predict what they think will happen and to write why they think their prediction is accurate. Allow them sufficient time to write before you ask them to share their predictions and their reasoning behind those predictions with the class. Write students' ideas on the board so that the entire class can see. Then carry out the demonstration and allow students time again to record

Table 7.1   Planning Process for POE Formative Assessments

Step 1: Setting Learning Goals	
Science content	What standards-based understandings will your POE address? Think not only about content-based standards but also about which understandings about inquiry the activity might target.
Supporting learning goal	What do you want students to know and be able to do?
Step 2: Finding Out What Students Know	
Assessment purpose	What is the purpose of this activity, and why is it being placed at this point in the unit?
Placement in unit	What is happening in the unit before and after the students complete the POE?
Assessment activity	What exactly will be demonstrated? What information will students be given before they make their predictions? What exactly will students predict?
Data to be collected about student learning	How will the students share their understanding: through a vote, by sharing ideas at tables before sharing with the whole class, or in a whole-class discussion where students volunteer their answers?
Step 3: Anticipating Feedback	
Probable student alternative conceptions	What are the common misunderstandings, prior beliefs, or misconceptions that students might draw upon?
Feedback ideas	What activities might students complete to help them see that prior understandings are not as accurate as the scientific explanation you expect them to reach?

their responses to the demonstration. Holding a second discussion at this point will provide students with the opportunity to bring the evidence they have just observed to bear on the explanations they have proposed. Figure 7.1 illustrates the sequence of these different strategies and the level of the classroom organization in which it should take place (with either the whole class or individual students).

As students are sharing their ideas, think about the present state of their understanding with respect to what it is you want them to learn. Are their predictions accurate? What do their predictions reveal about the state of their thinking? Are they based on the prior ideas and alternative conceptions that you were expecting? The information you collect from them is both general and specific. You will get a general idea of what students know based on their ability to predict what will happen. If these predictions fall into only

Figure 7.1   Sequence for Enacting POE Formative Assessments

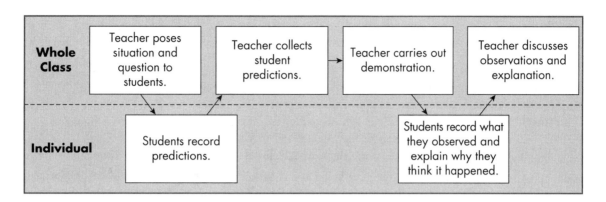

two or three possible categories, you may want the students to vote so you can get a good *ballpark* idea of what they are thinking. The specific information comes when the students are asked to provide explanations for their ideas. You may want to write down what students say either on the board or on an overhead projector. Look for and mark similarities between students' explanations, writing these ideas together to reinforce that there are many different ways of saying the same thing. When students' ideas differ, ask them to share the evidence or reasons they have for their explanations, and promote argumentation by asking students to react to each other's predictions.

POE EXAMPLE 7.1: SINKING AND FLOATING

Step 1: Setting Learning Goals	
Science content	The National Science Education Standards for Physical Science in Grades 5–8 state that students should build understandings of the characteristic properties of substances, including their density. The Grades 5–8 standard for understandings about scientific inquiry states that students should develop explanations that emphasize evidence and use scientific principles, models, and theories.
Supporting learning goal	The students will come to know that whether an object will sink or float in a given liquid depends on the ratio of the density of the object to the density of the liquid. If the density of the object is greater than the density of the liquid, the object will sink; if the density of the object is less than the density of the liquid, it will float.

(Continued)

(Continued)

Step 2: Finding Out What Students Know	
Assessment purpose	This activity is designed to elicit students' explanations about sinking and floating in a demonstration involving variables that they have not yet worked with in class.
Placement in unit	Middle school students have completed several investigations examining the variables involved in sinking and floating, including density, but they have placed objects only in water. This task extends the idea of relative density as a cause for sinking or floating by presenting students with a different liquid. Students are asked to make a prediction as to whether the new liquid will have an effect on the sinking or floating of the block. Then, students will complete a series of investigations in which they explore the densities of liquids.
Assessment activity	Students make a prediction about what will happen when a block is placed in a beaker of isopropyl alcohol. They are asked to give reasons for their predictions. When the teacher places the block in the alcohol, the block sinks even though it floated in water; students are then asked to provide an explanation for what they observed.
Data to be collected about student learning	Students' votes on whether the block will sink or float in isopropyl alcohol and students' explanations for their predictions.
Step 3: Anticipating Feedback	
Probable student alternative conceptions	There are *sinking* objects and *floating* objects, and whether these objects will sink or float is independent of the liquid in which they are placed; objects with a density greater than one will sink in any liquid; thick liquids may *stick* to the object and change its depth of sinking.
Feedback ideas	Students who think that a given object will sink or float should be given multiple examples of objects and liquids and allowed to explore the effects different liquids have on whether objects will sink or float (possible liquids to use might be saltwater, oil, or isopropyl alcohol). Students who think that liquids will stick to objects might find the density of these objects before and after they have been submerged in the liquid to see how the density of the objects remains unchanged.

Science Content Standard is from National Research Council. (1996). *National Science Education Standards.* Washington, DC: National Academies Press.

PREDICT-OBSERVE-EXPLAIN: SINKING AND FLOATING

Name: _____

Date: _____ Period: _____

The teacher has a block of a density of 0.95 g/cm³ and a beaker filled with isopropyl alcohol.

Figure 7.2 Block and Alcohol POE Setup _____

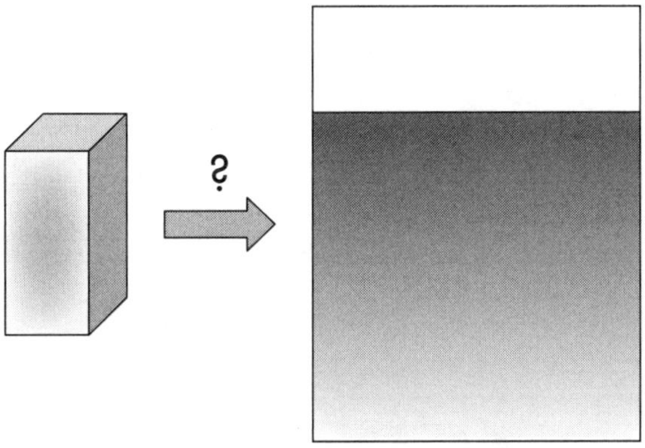

What will happen when the teacher places the block in the isopropyl alcohol? Predict whether this block will sink, float, or subsurface float.

I predict that the block will _____ in isopropyl alcohol.

I predict this because

Observe as your teacher places the block into the saltwater. What did you observe? Why?

Source: Stanford Education Assessment Laboratory. (2003). *Teacher's Guide to the Reflective Lessons.* Unpublished manuscript

Formative Assessment in Action: POE

Ms. McDonald and her sixth-grade physical science students are toward the end of a multiple-week inquiry-based unit about density and buoyancy. Her students have worked in groups to investigate the effects of mass, volume, and density on the ability of different objects to sink or float in water and have participated in many class discussions to try to develop a universal explanation for sinking and floating. So far, students have come to the conclusion that objects with a density greater than one will sink in water, objects with a density of one will have neutral buoyancy, and objects with a density of less than one will float in water.

Now, Ms. McDonald wants to help her students to make the transition from thinking about density and sinking and floating only in water to a more general understanding of comparing the density of an object to the density of the liquid in which it is placed. Before doing so, Ms. McDonald wants to stop and check to see if her students can predict whether an object will sink or float in water based on information about its density.

Ms. McDonald hands out the sinking and floating POE to her students. She starts by filling a beaker with water and asking students, given the information about the density of the block, to predict what will happen when it is placed in water. The majority of students vote that the block will float; one student votes that it will sink.

Ms. McDonald: So its density is 0.95. And I just filled this with water. This is just what we talked about before. We know the density of the object; we've been dealing with water, so I'm going to put it in, and we're going to see what happens. *[Drops block into the water; it floats.]* What's it doing?

Students: Floating.

Ms. McDonald: It's floating. Those of you who said "float," how did you know? How did you know? Trey?

Trey: Its density is under one?

Ms. McDonald: Yeah, well, let's look. Its density was less than one. It was 0.95. Density less than one, float.

In this exchange, Ms. McDonald took a hand vote to get a quick tally of how many of her students could correctly predict that the block with a density of 0.95 g/cm^3 would float in water. Once she saw that most of her students were able to make the right prediction, she quickly called on a student to share the explanation for this prediction. In this way, Ms. McDonald was able to check all of her students' understandings while also reinforcing the correct explanation by having Trey repeat it to the class. Ms. McDonald registered that one student did not predict accurately but did not decide to spend too much time singling this student out; she could easily speak with the student individually at a later time.

Ms. McDonald then moved onto a different context, replacing the water in the beaker with isopropyl alcohol.

Ms. McDonald: Now, we're using a different liquid. You already said that in water this was going to float because its density was less than one. Well, now I want to talk little bit about what if we don't use water? What if we use a different liquid? Will it have the same effect? Will it still float? Will it subsurface float, or will it sink?

After allowing students several minutes to make their predictions on the handout and write in their explanations, Ms. McDonald wanted to quickly find out what they had written, so she called for a vote.

Ms. McDonald: So how many people thought it would still float? Raise your hand. Still going to float. All right, floaters, why? Why do you think it's still going to float? Alex?

Alex: Because the density is still one.

Ms. McDonald: Because the density's still one. I haven't changed the density have I? Sorry. Under one. It's still less than one. Haven't done anything to change that, so he's saying it doesn't matter. The density of this is still under one; it's going to float. Okay. Someone else. Another floater. Another floater. Sasha?

Sasha: Density is still under one, and I think the different liquid won't have an effect because the mass didn't change, and the volume didn't change.

Ms. McDonald: All right, so you're saying that this is still the same. The mass isn't changing, the volume of it isn't changing, so she doesn't think the liquid will have any effect.

In this exchange, Ms. McDonald was able to identify at least two students—Alex and Sasha—who believed that the block would also float in alcohol because the block had not been changed. Ms. McDonald has gained the information about these students that they are not yet thinking about liquids as potentially having different densities and that those densities might have an effect on whether the block will sink or float.

Ms. McDonald: All right, what about you subsurface people? Who thought it would subsurface float? Oh, our lone soul. Rosa. Okay, Rosa, why do you think it's going to subsurface?

Rosa: I thought because it's a different liquid, it would add more mass.

Ms. McDonald: And what would make it add more mass? What do you think? All right, so she's saying that this liquid has something in it that water doesn't have. Like obviously, which one of these would I be able to drink?

Students: Water.

Ms. McDonald: So obviously there's something in here that makes it *bad*. So she's—what Rosa's—saying, and clarify for me if I'm wrong, is that whatever's added in here to make it bad will give this more mass, which would make it subsurface float. So why subsurface float, though?

Rosa: Because it might have a *little* bit more.

Ms. McDonald: Okay, not a lot, to make it go all the way down, but a little bit more. So if we're saying subsurface float, and this is 0.95, what would we have to say about this?

Rosa: It's the same.

Ms. McDonald: Okay, we would have to say it's the same. Because what do we know about subsurface floaters?

(Continued)

(Continued)

Rosa:	They're equal.
Ms. McDonald:	They're equal. The mass and volume is equal. All right. Thank you for being brave, Rosa.

When Ms. McDonald asked students to vote on whether the block would subsurface float, she had only one student make this prediction. Ms. McDonald was careful to reinforce Rosa's vote by thanking her for being brave and then was careful to ask Rosa to fully explain her reasoning for choosing that option. Here, Ms. McDonald gained information that Rosa believed that the different liquid had something additional in it that gave it more mass and that in turn would affect whether or not the block would sink or float; in Rosa's estimation, it would add just enough mass to make the block subsurface float.

Ms. McDonald then asked students to vote on the final option, the sinking block; about one third of the students raised their hands.

Ms. McDonald:	So sinkers, raise your hand if you think it would sink. All right, why? Zack, why do you think it's going to sink?
Zack:	If the liquid is denser than water, it would make it float, but maybe the different liquid would make it float more, higher than one.
Ms. McDonald:	So you're saying that you think this liquid has what would be higher than one? What is it called?
Zack:	Density.
Ms. McDonald:	It's density. So he's saying, "Wait a minute here, we cannot only be concerned with the density of this [block], but maybe the density of this [alcohol] is different."

Zack reveals here that he understands that the density of the alcohol might be different than that of the water even though his reasoning is inconsistent and should lead him to a conclusion that the block would float, not sink. Ms. McDonald registers this information by repeating Zack's reasoning back to him and then solicits other explanations.

Ms. McDonald:	Another sinker explanation. Jed?
Jed:	Maybe the liquid could have an effect on the block.
Ms. McDonald:	Okay, so again the liquid's going to have some kind of effect. Can you be more specific? What kind of effect do you think it's going to have?
Matt:	That it will make it sink.
Ms. McDonald:	That it will make it sink? What do you think? Who can help Matt? Why do you think? Anna, what can you add?
Anna:	Something has to be sticking to it and making it sink more.
Ms. McDonald:	Okay, so she's saying well, kind of what like Rosa said, even though Rosa thought it would subsurface float. There's something else in here, and if you add it to what Matt said, it adds more mass to it. It's a theory. Jed?
Jed:	The liquid's gonna add mass to it by sticking liquid on it and pulling it down.
Ms. McDonald:	Okay, so because it's a different liquid, you think it's going to stick a little more to it, which would give it mass.

Jed reveals to Ms. McDonald similar reasoning to what Rosa had thought, only he uses it to reach the conclusion that the block will sink instead of float.

Through this activity, which took about 10 minutes of class time, Ms. McDonald was able to check to see if most students could accurately predict what the block would do in water and then get information about the extent to which they could apply that information to alcohol. She learned that students were divided on what would happen, and even those who correctly predicted that the block would sink in water were not reasoning from the correct explanation. Ms. McDonald carried out the demonstration, and students spoke out in surprise when the block sank in the alcohol. She then used students' piqued interest as a result of this formative assessment to go straight into the next activity, which focused on relative density, bringing with her information about the status of students' learning.

Although Ms. McDonald was able to hear several students' explanations, a pitfall of relying only on students speaking in class is that all of her students did not speak, and given the way that students made their predictions, she knew that some students probably had different, possibly inaccurate ideas. Ms. McDonald collected the students' handouts and looked them over after class, not to grade them but to get a more representative sample of what *all* the students in her class were thinking.

Based on her classroom discussion and reading through students' responses, Ms. McDonald was able to determine that she would need to focus in the coming investigations on how liquids, like objects, have density, and on the fact that it is the ratio of the density of the object and liquid that determines whether the object sinks or floats. The coming investigations would allow students to investigate these properties, so Ms. McDonald planned to ask extra questions of those students who seemed confused about the effect the different liquid would have on the object's sinking or floating to make sure that they were coming to understand the ideas in the next supporting learning goal.

POE EXAMPLE 7.2: AIR PRESSURE

Step 1: Setting Learning Goals	
Science content	The Grades 9–12 National Science Education Standards for Physical Science state that students should understand that heat consists of random motion and the vibrations of atoms and molecules. In addition, the Grades 9–12 Earth and Space Science Standard for energy in the earth system states that students should know that the heating of the earth's atmosphere by the sun drives convection within the atmosphere, producing winds (National Research Council, 1996).
Supporting Learning Goal	The students will come to know that when air is heated, it expands and, consequently, becomes less dense. Some of this air escapes from the flask, causing the egg to wobble. This leads to the bottle being filled with hot, low-density air. When the fire goes out in the flask, the air cools. But because the egg is

(Continued)

(Continued)

	blocking the opening, the volume of air in the bottle stays the same. Since there is now less air in the bottle, the pressure in the bottle is less than before. So, there is unequal pressure between the air outside the flask and the air inside the flask. The greater pressure outside the flask pushes the egg into the flask, and the system returns to equilibrium.
Step 2: Finding Out What Students Know	
Assessment purpose	To determine whether students understand how air masses with high and low pressure move and create weather phenomena, the teacher carries out this formative assessment to determine if students can connect the motion of the egg to the differential pressure created by the heating of the air inside the flask.
Placement in unit	High school students are engaged in a unit on weather and the physical phenomena that create it. Air pressure is a concept that is often difficult for students to interpret; everyday language such as *sucking* is often used in situations rather than *differential pressure* (Driver, Guesne & Tiberghien, 1985).
Assessment activity	Students make a prediction as to what will happen when the air inside an Erlenmeyer flask is heated and a hardboiled egg is set on top. They are asked to give reasons for their predictions of what will happen. When the teacher carries out the demonstration, students will observe that the egg will first bounce on the top of the flask while heated air escapes; eventually, the air pressure inside the flask becomes sufficiently lower than the air pressure outside the flask, resulting in the egg being pushed into the flask. Students are then asked to explain what they have observed.
Data to be collected about student learning	Students' descriptions of what they expect to happen to the egg, as well as the explanations for their predictions
Step 3: Anticipating Feedback	
Probable student alternative conceptions	The atmosphere exerts pressure that is observable only when there is a difference in pressure; the atmosphere exerts pressure on all surfaces; vacuums *suck* or exert pressure; spaces must be filled; the pressure of air inside the flask sucks or pulls the egg into the flask (Driver, Guesne, & Tiberghien, 1985).
Feedback ideas	Since students commonly focus only on what is happening to the air inside the flask, the teacher should speak to them about equilibrium and help them to compare what is happening inside the flask with the air outside the flask.

Science Content Standard is from National Research Council. (1996). *National Science Education Standards.* Washington, DC: National Academies Press.

PREDICT-OBSERVE-EXPLAIN: EGG-IN-THE-FLASK

Name: _____

Date: _____ Period: _____

The teacher has an Erlenmeyer flask, a hardboiled egg, and a small piece of newspaper. The teacher will set the piece of paper on fire, drop it into the flask, and set the egg on top of the opening to the flask.

Figure 7.3 Egg and Flask POE Setup

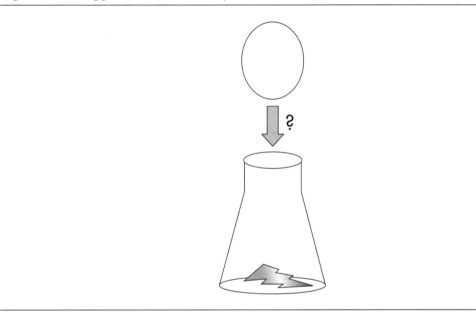

What do you think will happen when the teacher lights the paper on fire and places the egg on top of the flask?

I predict this because

Observe as your teacher lights the paper on fire and places the egg on top of the beaker. What did you observe? Why?

8

Evidence-to-Explanation Assessments

Chapter Overview

- **What is an evidence-to-explanation formative assessment?**
- **When should I use evidence-to-explanation assessments in my unit?**
- **How can I develop my own evidence-to-explanation assessments?**
- **How can I enact evidence-to-explanation assessments in my classroom?**
- **Evidence-to-explanation example 8.1: Natural selection**
  - **Formative assessment in action: Darwin's finches on the Galapagos Islands**
- **Evidence-to-explanation example 8.2: Phase changes in water**

WHAT IS AN EVIDENCE-TO-EXPLANATION FORMATIVE ASSESSMENT?

One of the major themes in recent science education reform is that students should be able to evaluate the quality of scientific evidence and develop explanations on the basis of that evidence. According to *Inquiry and the*

National Science Education Standards (National Research Council, 2001), students should be able to do the following:

- Give priority to evidence in responding to questions
- Formulate explanations from evidence
- Connect explanations to scientific knowledge

Similarly, Richard Duschl writes, "Science at its core is fundamentally about acquiring data and then transforming that data first into evidence and then into explanations" (Duschl, 2003, p. 47). In order for students to be able to develop explanations on the basis of evidence, they need to be able to examine scientific evidence, understand what it means, and connect it to their explanations.

One kind of formative assessment attempts to do this by presenting students with data and asking them to use it to support a scientific explanation. These assessments, which I call "evidence-to-explanation" assessments, place several different kinds of demands on students. First, students need to be able to simply read the graph or figure that they are being provided. Second, they need to draw on the science concepts they have learned in class to be able to properly interpret the evidence the graph or figure contains. Third, they need to be able to formulate an explanation that combines the evidence provided in the assessment with their knowledge. The way that students respond to these assessments will reveal gaps in their reasoning and provide you with information about which elements may need to be revisited to help students reach learning goals.

WHEN SHOULD I USE EVIDENCE-TO-EXPLANATION ASSESSMENTS IN MY UNIT?

Evidence-to-explanation assessments combine students' interpretation skills with content understanding, so they should be placed after students have acquired both of those skills in a unit. For example, reading certain kinds of diagrams or graphs takes practice, so giving a formative assessment that contains a Punnett square before students have learned to read one will frustrate them and will likely yield little more than a set of "I don't know" responses. However, after students have learned how to read and make Punnett squares, asking them to create or interpret a new one will help them employ and build on their new knowledge. Thus, the best place to use these assessments is when you want to check whether students have learned how to interpret a new kind of evidence and whether they can apply their conceptual knowledge to the information they get from the evidence they are interpreting.

HOW CAN I DEVELOP MY OWN EVIDENCE-TO-EXPLANATION ASSESSMENTS?

Assessments that involve graphs, tables, or figures can often be answered without any prerequisite scientific knowledge. Take, for example, the following question from the Trends in International Mathematics and Science Study (TIMSS) eighth-grade assessment:

The table gives the temperature at a certain place at different times of the day for three days.

	6 a.m.	9 a.m.	12 noon	3 p.m.	6 p.m.
Monday	15°C	17°C	20°C	21°C	19°C
Tuesday	15°C	15°C	14°C	5°C	4°C
Wednesday	8°C	10°C	14°C	14°C	13°C

When did the wind become much colder?

A. Monday morning

B. Monday afternoon

C. Tuesday morning

D. Tuesday afternoon

E. Wednesday afternoon

Source: National Center for Education Statistics, U.S. Department of Education.

TIMSS categorizes this problem in the domain of reasoning and analysis. In order to answer the question correctly, students need to understand that "become much colder" means "decrease in temperature," and after examining all of the data, a student can quickly deduce that the temperature became much colder Tuesday afternoon at 3 p.m. and select answer D.

There are several characteristics of this problem that make it different from an evidence-to-explanation assessment. Students do not need in-depth conceptual knowledge to respond to this problem, and they are not asked to synthesize their knowledge with the data presented in the table at all. Furthermore, the problem is multiple choice, and so the cognitive demand the question puts on students is lower; they can simply select an answer and move to the next question rather than composing an interpretation of the evidence and an explanation based on it (e.g., the biggest decrease in the temperature happened on Tuesday at 3 p.m.; therefore, the wind must have become colder at that time).

Contrast the weather question with the one that follows, adapted from an example in the textbook *BSCS Biology: An Ecological Approach* (Biological Sciences Curriculum Study, 2006):

There are three kinds of phenotypes in morning glory flowers: red, white, and pink. A scientist performed crosses across three generations of morning glories and obtained the following results:

Figure 8.1 Phenotypes in Morning Glory Flowers

P_1 Red —x— White

F_1 Pink —x— Pink

F_2 Red   Pink   Pink   White

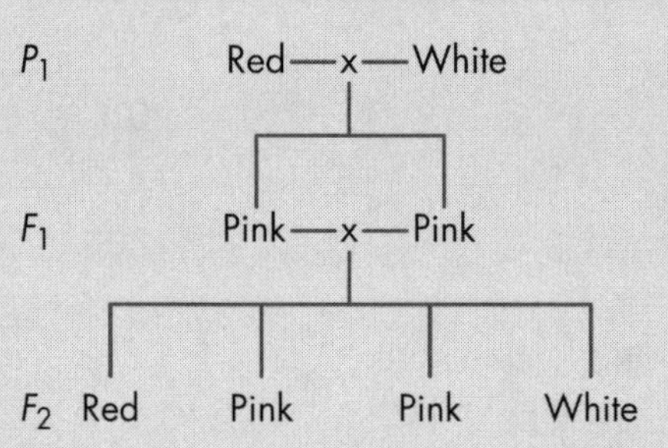

Based on what you know about alleles and phenotypes, what can you say about the gene that controls flower color in morning glories? How do you know?

Source: Based on Biological Sciences Curriculum Study. (2006). *BSCS Biology: An Ecological Approach* (10th ed.). Dubuque, IA: Kendall/Hunt.

Like the weather question, the morning glory example above asks students to evaluate evidence provided in a table or figure. Unlike the weather question, however, the morning glory question cannot be interpreted without significant prior knowledge about genes and patterns of inheritance. First, the students need to understand what an allele and a phenotype are and then be able to interpret the information given in the figure (P_1, F_1, etc.). The figure shows that a white flower crossed with a red flower gives two pink flowers and that those two flowers crossed will produce a red, two pinks, and one white flower. This indicates that individual flowers with one red gene and one white gene will produce a pink flower, an instance of codominance. In order to answer this question, then, students need to draw upon their prior knowledge of genotypes and phenotypes, dominant and recessive genes, and codominance to interpret the figure and to develop an explanation of why the given phenotypes result from these crosses.

I provided these two examples to illustrate how evidence-to-explanation assessments go beyond simple interpretation of graphs that can often be done in the absence of conceptual understanding. In contrast, evidence-to-explanation assessments are designed to help students combine their conceptual understanding with their ability to interpret tables, graphs, and figures to formulate a scientific explanation. Evidence-to-explanation assessments thus have three characteristics:

1. They include some kind of evidence to interpret, in the form of a figure, table, or graph.

2. Interpreting the evidence requires both interpretation skills and conceptual understanding.

3. Students must combine information from the evidence with conceptual understanding to formulate an explanation.

To write your own evidence-to-explanation formative assessment, begin with the planning sheet for formative assessment. I've written specific prompts to help you prepare specifically for evidence-to-explanation assessments in Table 8.1.

Table 8.1 Planning Process for Evidence-to-Explanation Formative Assessments

Step 1: Setting Learning Goals	
Science content	What standard will you be addressing with the formative assessment?
Supporting learning goal	What standards-based conceptual understandings are you trying to assess? What kind of evidence (figure, table, or graph) is both a good representation of the content and a basis for asking an explanation-type question?
Step 2: Finding Out What Students Know	
Assessment purpose	What is the purpose of having students interpret this graph?
Placement in unit	What is happening in the unit before and after the students complete the evidence-to-explanation assessment?
Assessment activity	What is the nature of the data that will be included in the graph? Will students have seen this graph or one like it before, or will it be completely new to them? What information needs to accompany the graph in order for students to interpret it? What is the interpretation that you are looking for?
Data to be collected about student learning	Once students have interpreted the graph and provided an explanation, how will they demonstrate their understanding to you?
Step 3: Anticipating Feedback	
Probable student alternative conceptions	In what ways might students misinterpret or misunderstand the evidence? What are the common misunderstandings, prior beliefs, or alternative conceptions that students might use to explain the evidence?
Feedback ideas	What activities might help students develop the conceptual understanding necessary to provide the correct explanation for the evidence they have been provided?

Now that you have your plan, it's time to find the evidence that your students will interpret. Starting with your learning goal, look for graphs, tables, and figures in textbooks, the Internet, science magazines, and released test items. The important thing to remember when selecting a graph, table, or figure is that the evidence being presented should require students to draw on prior conceptual knowledge.

Once you have your evidence for students to interpret, think of a question that will help focus students on your learning goal. In the morning glory example above, students are asked to draw on their prior knowledge about alleles and phenotypes to describe the observed colors in these flowers.

HOW CAN I ENACT EVIDENCE-TO-EXPLANATION ASSESSMENTS IN MY CLASSROOM?

Of course, the simplest and most straightforward way to implement evidence-to-explanation assessments is to have individual students complete them and then collect and read them later. My prior research has shown that this is the most accurate way to find out what your students know (Furtak & Ruiz-Primo, 2008); however, to complete the feedback loop, you would also have to write comments on each student's work, speak personally to each student about how to improve his or her responses, or speak to the class about common mistakes after reading through the papers.

A different way of approaching evidence-to-explanation assessments is to take the opportunity to engage students in what Duschl (2003) called the *social* domain of inquiry, where students explore evidence and talk about what it might mean. To do so, you may place your students in small groups after they have responded to the evidence-to-explanation assessments on their own and ask them to talk about the concepts underlying the evidence and how that relates to their explanation. By assembling these groups in a heterogeneous manner, you can even the playing field in your classroom and allow students to draw on each other's expertise (Cohen, 1994). Peers with a clearer understanding can help students confused by the evidence, and the explainers in turn will benefit by learning how to explain the evidence to their peers.

Once students come to agreement on their interpretation, they can turn to talking about what the table, graph, or figure means in the context of the question posed by the assessment before reporting their results to the larger class. In this way, you will engage students in the interpretation of evidence and the transformation of evidence into explanations, a truly authentic inquiry experience. At the same time, you will find out what students know and help students benefit from each other's expertise. Figure 8.2 illustrates the sequence of these steps and the level of the classroom organization in which each should take place.

As students are speaking in groups, don't forget to listen to each group as they discuss the evidence and explanations. Listen to determine if

Figure 8.2 Sequence for Enacting Evidence-to-Explanation Formative Assessments

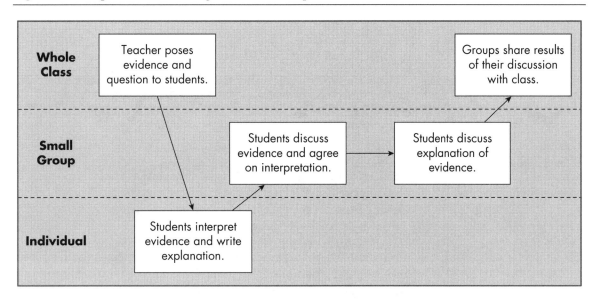

students are drawing upon the conceptual knowledge they need to interpret the evidence and to see if the explanations the students are developing are appropriate. You may have to remind some groups that they should agree on what the evidence means before proceeding to the next step. Also, listening to students speak in small groups will help you come to understand which of your students are having difficulty interpreting the graphs, an important piece of information since students speaking before the class can be more likely to give the correct interpretation (Furtak & Ruiz-Primo, 2008).

As you plan your evidence-to-explanation assessment, use the examples at the end of this chapter as a guide, and remember to use Planning Sheet G included in the Resources section at the end of the book.

EVIDENCE-TO-EXPLANATION EXAMPLE 8.1: NATURAL SELECTION

Step 1: Setting Learning Goals	
Science content	The National Science Education Standards' Life Sciences Content Standard C for students in Grades 9–12 states, "Species evolve over time. Evolution is the consequence of the interactions of (1) the potential for a species to increase its numbers, (2) the genetic variability of offspring due to mutation and recombination of genes, (3) a finite supply of the resources required for life, and (4) the ensuing selection by the environment of those offspring better able to survive and leave offspring."

(Continued)

(Continued)

Supporting learning goal	The students will be able to explain that there was variation in the beak size of this population of finches before the drought, but afterward, only certain finches survived to reproduce. These finches had beaks of a certain size that were more effective at cracking the large, hard seeds that were left over after all the other seeds had been eaten.
Step 2: Finding Out What Students Know	
Assessment purpose	The purpose is to determine whether or not students can apply the theory of natural selection to interpret a set of real data.
Context	This formative assessment should be implemented late in a unit when students have learned about the different facts and inferences associated with natural selection and now have an opportunity to bring those pieces together to interpret a graph.
Assessment activity	Data from the graph is taken from Peter and Rosemary Grant's research on Darwin's finches on the Galapagos Islands. While students may have been exposed to the story of Darwin's finches, they probably have not seen these exact data. What information needs to accompany the graph in order for students to interpret it? What is the interpretation that you are looking for?
Data to be collected about student learning	Data about student learning is collected individually; students respond on a separate page and turn their assessments in to the teacher.
Step 3: Anticipating Feedback	
Probable student alternative conceptions	Students often think that changes in the environment cause changes in organisms; that is, organisms actively adapt to their environment. Students may also respond to the question without actually providing a mechanism for how natural selection occurs (Anderson, Fisher, & Norman, 2002).
Feedback ideas	Since students often think that changes in a population are caused by a changing environment rather than seeing that the differences in the population come from within the existing population, it would be useful to discuss each graph one at a time, highlighting the distribution of beak sizes and then helping students to see that certain finches with certain-sized beaks were more successful at cracking harder seeds. Then, in the second graph, only certain finches survived.

Science Content Standards are from National Research Council. (1996). *National Science Education Standards.* Washington, DC: National Academies Press, p. 185.

EVIDENCE-TO-EXPLANATION: NATURAL SELECTION

Name: _____

Date: _____ Period: _____

Peter and Rosemary Grant are biologists who have spent every summer since 1973 doing research into finches that live on a tiny island in the Galapagos. Each year, they catch hundreds of these birds and make many measurements of them, including their weight and size, as well as observing the kinds of seeds the birds are eating. The finches' body size and the size and shape of their beaks vary depending on what kind of seeds they eat.

In 1977, there was a harsh drought on the Galapagos Islands, causing the plants to shrivel and die. This meant that there were fewer seeds for the finches to eat. First, the birds ate the small, soft seeds, leaving only large and tough seeds to eat—seeds that the finches usually did not eat.

The two graphs below illustrate the Grants' data collected in 1976 and 1978, the years before and after the 1977 drought.

Figure 8.3 Data From Galapagos Finches

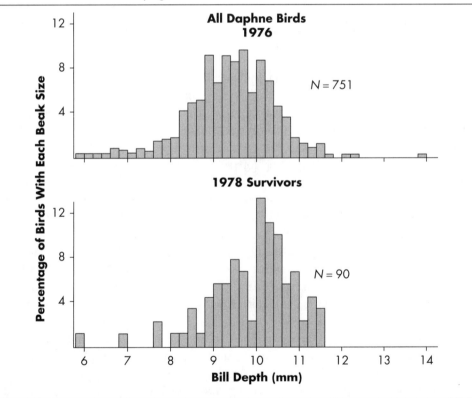

Source: Grant, Peter R. *Ecology and Evolution of Darwin's Finches.* © 1986 Princeton University Press. Reprinted by permission of Princeton University Press.

What do the two graphs above illustrate about natural selection? Be sure to refer to specific evidence from the graphs in your answer.

Source: WGBH Educational Foundation and Clear Blue Sky Productions, Inc. (2001). *Finch Beak Data Sheet,* downloaded July 1, 2007, from http://www.pbs.org/wgbh/evolution/library/01/6/l_016_01.html.

Formative Assessment in Action:
Darwin's Finches on the Galapagos Islands

Mr. Solano had almost finished teaching his tenth-grade general biology students about natural selection and wanted to know if his students would be able to put together all the pieces they had learned. After an online search, he found some information about Peter and Rosemary Grant's famous research on Darwin's finches on the Galapagos Islands and adapted the information he found into a formative assessment for his students. He adapted a bit of the accompanying text into background information and then cut and pasted the graphs below it. He then posed a question in which students were asked to apply the information in the graph to a larger idea about natural selection.

Since Mr. Solano had held several class discussions during his Evolution unit, he wanted to give students a chance to respond individually to the formative assessment. This way, he knew he would find out what *all* his students knew—not just those who spoke most often in the class. He introduced the formative assessment by telling students he wanted to see them apply what they had learned to some real data collected in the Galapagos Islands and encouraged students to respond to the question as completely and clearly as they could. Mr. Solano let his students know that he wanted them to work individually since he wanted to find out what the students knew themselves. He emphasized that their responses would not be graded but would be used to help him plan the last few lessons in the unit.

Mr. Solano then handed out the assessments and gave students about 15 minutes to write their responses. A few students had trouble understanding the way the graphs were labeled, and a few of his English language learners needed help understanding some of the words in the background information above the graphs like *finches* and *shrivel*.

When enough time had passed for each student to write something in response to the assessment, Mr. Solano picked up each student's work and thanked each for his or her effort. "I'm looking forward to reading these this afternoon to see what you've learned," he said with a smile.

After school, Mr. Solano poured himself a cup of coffee and sat at his desk to read through his students' responses. To his dismay, several students had left the response completely blank or had written something short such as, "This demonstrates natural selection because after the drought it shows birds' beaks depth getting larger. Since the environment is changing, the birds have to adapt to their new surroundings."

Based on responses like these, Mr. Solano realized that he needed to revise the evidence-to-explanation assessment for next year to reduce the reading load for his students with low proficiency in English, as well as to make the graphs clearer overall.

Two of Mr. Solano' students gave responses that he felt had the right idea and definitely related the evidence from the graph to explanations, as illustrated by the response in Figure 8.4. However, Mr. Solano noticed that many of his students interpreted the graph as showing that the finches' beaks changed to adapt to the environment (Rudolph & Stewart, 1998). Two of these responses are shown in Figures 8.5 and 8.6.

A few other students had given responses that used words they had learned in class but in unclear ways. In Figure 8.7, the student uses *adapt* and *getting larger* without stating how that happens.

Based on this information, Mr. Solano knew that he needed to address the common misunderstanding that this graph reflected changes in the finches that had been caused by the environment. He planned to talk specifically about the graph the next day and to invite students to talk about the mechanism underlying the changes between the first and second graphs. In the first graph, there is a clear distribution in the size of the finches' beaks, and the y-axis has much higher numbers of individuals than the second graph. Highlighting these differences and then helping students to visualize the finches' experiences in a drought could help students better understand that the change in the distribution of the finches could be attributed to the differential success of finches with a particular beak size.

Figure 8.4   Evidence-to-Explanation: Student Response 1

The data in the two graphs above illustrates the difference between the ideal beak sizes for birds on the Galapagos Islands from before and after the drought. Before the drought of 1977, birds with beak sizes of 9-11 mm were commonly prominent. This showed natural selection because these birds had the largest population. However, after the drought, the group of large population birds that had good beak sizes had gaps. Birds with beak depths sized 9.¹ - 9.⁹, 10.² - 11.⁵ thrived, but there were gaps between the groups.

Figure 8.5   Evidence-to-Explanation: Student Response 2

It shows that when food and other resources become scarce, the finches develop over a period of time different beaks to eat the hard seeds that seem to be abundant.

Figure 8.6   Evidence-to-Explanation: Student Response 3

Since the drought occured the new offspring of Daphne birds had smaller beaks. They had to change thy physical opperences in order to survive.

Figure 8.7   Evidence-to-Explanation: Student Response 4

This demonstrates natural seclection because after the drought it shows birds beaks depth getting larger. Since the enviorment is changing the birds have to adapt to their new surroundings.

(Continued)

(Continued)

In addition, Mr. Solano realized that, judging by the students' answers, asking them to jump directly to an explanation of the graph might be too large a step to make. He considered that he should give the assessment again with another question asking students for some specific information from the graph so that in the next question they could focus on interpreting the graph in terms of what it meant about natural selection. In order to gauge whether students were making progress toward the learning goal, Mr. Solano planned to give the modified version of the assessment later in the unit to see if his students' responses improved as a result of more instruction and the revised questions. In addition, Mr. Solano planned to give his students additional formative assessments that get at the same idea of how natural selection works to determine whether the assessment itself was impeding his ability to find out what students knew or if his students truly needed more experience with the evidence for evolution before proceeding in the unit.

EVIDENCE-TO-EXPLANATION
EXAMPLE 8.2: PHASE CHANGES IN WATER

Step 1: Setting Learning Goals	
Science content	The National Science Education Standards' Content Standards for Physical Science in Grades 5–8 state that students should understand that substances have characteristic properties such as density and boiling point.
Supporting learning goal	The students will come to know that the temperature at which water boils (represented by the plateau on the diagram) will not be influenced by an increase in the amount of mass being heated; however, the amount of time and energy it takes to boil the water will increase because more energy is needed to heat the increased mass.
Step 2: Finding Out What Students Know	
Assessment purpose	The purpose is to find out if students understand the patterns in temperature changes when heat energy is added or removed and can connect those patterns to observable phase changes.
Placement in unit	Students will have taken measurements of temperature versus time during laboratory investigations to create phase change diagrams for several substances, including water, that have different specific heat capacities. However, the way that phase change diagrams change when the amount of matter being heated is increased or decreased may not have been explicitly addressed in the curriculum, so this formative assessment represents a stretch for students to apply what they know about boiling point (i.e., when there is sufficient energy being added to break water molecules free to become water vapor) to the amount of water being heated (American Chemical Society, 2007).

Assessment activity	The students will be presented an unlabeled phase change diagram for water. Students will be asked how this phase change diagram would change if the amount of water being heated were doubled and then asked to explain why.
Data to be collected about student learning	Students will be asked to sketch on the graph how they think the line would change when the mass of water being heated is doubled, and then to explain why they think this will happen in the space provided below the graph.
Step 3: Anticipating Feedback	
Probable student alternative conceptions	Students may assume that an increase in mass implies an increase in the boiling point (Borsese, Lumbaca, & Pentimalli, 1996).
Feedback ideas	Ask students to explore the phenomenon by performing their own experiment to test the scientific explanation. Similarly, appealing to students' everyday experience can also help. Ask students, "How long does it take to boil a small pot of water, as compared to a gigantic pot of water keeping the stove range at the same setting?" In addition, describing how more energy is required to break intermolecular hydrogen bonds between water molecules can also help students to better understand the mechanism behind the observed difference between the two phase change diagrams.

Science Content Standards are from National Research Council. (1996). *National Science Education Standards.* Washington, DC: National Academies Press.

EVIDENCE-TO-EXPLANATION: PHASE CHANGES IN WATER

Name: _____

Date: _____ Period: _____

The diagram below illustrates the phase changes in water when energy is added to the system at a constant rate.

Figure 8.8   Water Phase Change Diagram

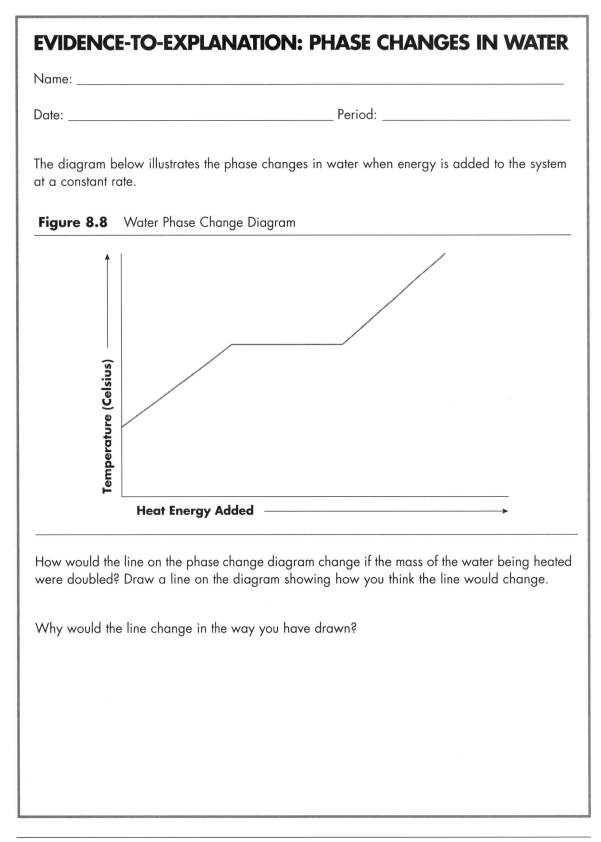

How would the line on the phase change diagram change if the mass of the water being heated were doubled? Draw a line on the diagram showing how you think the line would change.

Why would the line change in the way you have drawn?

9

Multiple-Choice Questions

WHAT IS A MULTIPLE-CHOICE FORMATIVE ASSESSMENT?

Formative assessment might not be the first thing to come to your mind upon hearing the phrase "multiple-choice question." These days, the phrase more likely makes you think of high-stakes tests and everything that comes with them: teacher and student anxiety, filling out endless rows and columns of bubbles, silent classrooms, and the scratching of freshly sharpened number two pencils. However, multiple-choice questions have probably gotten a bad rap because they are not all created equal, nor are they exclusively appropriate for summative assessment.

Traditional multiple-choice questions found on high-stakes summative assessments are often designed to test students' ability to recall facts, and the possible responses include one correct answer and a collection of incorrect answers. Take, for example, the following question, released from the National Assessment of Educational Progress (NAEP), which was given to students across the United States in 2005:

In your body, what two organs work together to make sure that oxygen gets to all the other organs of your body?

A. Lungs and kidneys

B. Heart and lungs

C. Brain and kidneys

D. Heart and liver

Source: National Center for Education Statistics, U.S. Department of Education

---

This question, classified by NAEP as *easy*, checks whether or not students know a fact: that the heart and lungs work together to get oxygen to the body. The incorrect options are combinations of organs that make little sense in terms of students' common misunderstandings of how oxygen gets into the body. Therefore, students who pick one answer or another simply have it *wrong*, and their decision to choose one of those responses in itself does not tell the teacher anything useful.

Multiple-choice questions can be specifically designed to provide information about what students know when each of the *incorrect* responses is linked to students' prior ideas or misunderstandings about the topic at hand. The alternative responses—sometimes called *distractors*—are what give this kind of question formative assessment power and distinguish it from multiple-choice questions that typically appear on summative assessments. The advantage of multiple-choice questions for formative assessment is twofold: First, the teacher gets to know which students have chosen which response, thereby quickly classifying students' understanding into categories that can be linked with activities to help students develop more scientific understandings. Second, the teacher can ask students to have conversations about which answer is best, forcing students to argue different points and bring evidence to bear on which scientific explanations are the most accurate.

It's true that using multiple-choice questions for formative assessment will keep your students' responses within a limited range of options, thus sacrificing some information that could give you further insight into student thinking. However, when you're teaching a class of 30 students, it's sometimes better to force students to choose from a list of responses. Multiple-choice questions actually have a distinct advantage over other types of formative assessments because they are able to exactly pinpoint students' understandings in a way that open-response and other unstructured assessments cannot. Students sort themselves into categories rather than leaving it incumbent on the teacher to do so with their responses.

Take, for example, the following question developed by Philip Sadler (1998, pp. 275–276):

The main reason for it being hotter in summer than in winter is

A. The earth's distance from the sun changes.

B. The sun is higher in the sky.

C. The distance between the northern hemisphere and the sun changes.

D. Ocean currents carry warm water north.

E. An increase occurs in "greenhouse gases."

Source: From Sadler, P. M. (1998). Psychometric models of student conceptions in science: Reconciling qualitative studies and distractor-driven assessment instruments. *Journal of Research in Science Teaching, 35*(3), 265–296.

Sadler found that only 12% of students in Grades 8–12 responding to this question chose B, the scientifically correct response. Distractors A and C were much more popular choices among students because each is linked to a common misunderstanding about why the seasons change on earth. Since many students believe that the earth's orbit is very irregular—a misconception arguably generated by perspective drawings in science textbooks that show the earth orbiting the sun from the side—they think that the sun is much closer to the earth in the summer than in the winter, making it warmer (A). A more accurate but still not entirely correct response (C) has to do with the tilt of the earth on its axis, causing it to lean toward the sun in the summer and away from the sun in the winter, but this is also not the actual cause for the seasons. The correct response, B, is based on the correlated influence of the tilt of the earth's axis and the resulting angle at which the rays of the sun reach the earth. The orientation of the earth's axis allows light to reach the surface at angles closer to 90 degrees, and this increased intensity makes the earth warmer during particular parts of the year. This question is one of many coming from a set called Distractor-Driven Multiple-Choice Questions (DDMCs), assembled into a test to explore students' understanding of important astronomy concepts (Sadler, 1998). Other tests like this exist as well. For example, in physics, there is the Force-Concept Inventory (FCI), a test specifically designed to identify misconceptions students have about kinematics and Newton's laws of motion (Hestenes, Wells, & Swackhamer, 1992). Each of the 29 questions on the FCI has distractors linked to students' common misconceptions, and the student's overall pattern of responses can provide useful information to a teacher about what students know. The patterns of responses that emerge from this sample of questions reveal a lot about what a student is thinking. Take the following question from the FCI as an example:

The positions of two blocks at successive 0.20-second time intervals are represented by the numbered squares in the figure below. The blocks are moving toward the right.

Figure 9.1   Blocks Question From the Force Concept Inventory

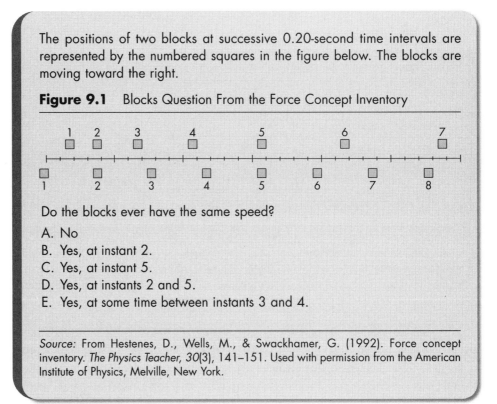

Do the blocks ever have the same speed?

A. No
B. Yes, at instant 2.
C. Yes, at instant 5.
D. Yes, at instants 2 and 5.
E. Yes, at some time between instants 3 and 4.

Source: From Hestenes, D., Wells, M., & Swackhamer, G. (1992). Force concept inventory. *The Physics Teacher, 30*(3), 141–151. Used with permission from the American Institute of Physics, Melville, New York.

This question is designed to get at students' common misconception that moving objects at the same position have the same speed. A student with this misconception would pick answer B, that the blocks have the same speed at instant 2; answer C, at instant 5; or answer D (both):

Figure 9.2   Illustration of Student Misconception That Moving Objects at the Same Position Have the Same Speed

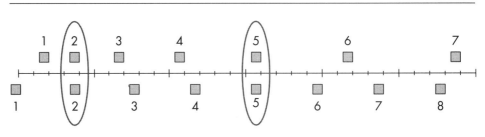

Source: Hestenes, D., Wells, M., & Swackhamer, G. (1992). Force concept inventory. *The Physics Teacher, 30*(3), 141–151. Used with permission from the American Institute of Physics, Melville, New York.

On the other hand, a student with a scientifically accurate understanding would look at the problem in a completely different way. These students know that speed means the distance traveled in an amount of time and so would look for similar distances covered by the blocks in .20-second intervals and select answer E:

Figure 9.3 Correct Student Response

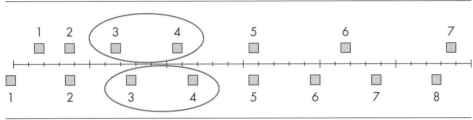

Source: Hestenes, D., Wells, M., & Swackhamer, G. (1992). Force concept inventory. *The Physics Teacher, 30*(3), 141–151. Used with permission from the American Institute of Physics, Melville, New York.

Thus, a teacher asking students to respond to a question like this will gain information about students' accurate understandings or persistent misconceptions based on which response each one chooses. If the question were given to students prior to a unit, and most selected answers B, C, or D, then the teacher would know that this particular understanding would need to be explored and directly addressed during instruction. If the teacher obtained the same results after an activity in which this concept had been explored, then the teacher would know that students need more practice and further instruction.

To sum up, multiple-choice questions for formative assessment have four characteristics. They are the following:

1. Linked to big idea questions

2. Written clearly and in language that is easy for your students to understand

3. Include one alternative response that is the scientifically correct explanation

4. Include a set of distractors that are linked to students' common prior ideas and misconceptions about the big idea being taught

Now let's turn to where, how, and when to use these formative assessments.

WHEN SHOULD I USE MULTIPLE-CHOICE QUESTIONS IN MY UNIT?

Multiple-choice questions work very well as preassessment tools or as embedded assessments linked to supporting learning goals in instructional units. As a preassessment tool, a small collection of high-quality distractor-driven questions can provide the teacher with valuable information about what students already know when they are beginning a unit so that instruction can be planned accordingly. As comprehension checks, multiple-choice questions can be used as warm-up activities at the beginning of class periods to review important concepts or at the conclusion of laboratory activities to check for common misunderstandings that may not have been directly addressed by students' activities.

HOW CAN I DEVELOP MY OWN MULTIPLE-CHOICE QUESTIONS?

A good multiple-choice question is very challenging to write because the distractors need to reflect students' thinking and be worded in terms that they would use. For every question that ends up on a standardized test, many more are discarded. Those that make the cut are extensively vetted and revised before they are considered statistically reliable. While multiple-choice questions for formative assessment in the classroom do not need to go through such an arduous development process before use, they still need to be clearly written and feature distractors linked to students' prior ideas and common misunderstandings. This requires extensive research or experience on the part of the question writer. To get started, you might be better served to look for questions that other people have written, evaluate whether they might serve a formative assessment purpose, and make small changes if needed to align the questions with students' common ideas and your own learning goals. In this section, I'll first talk about how to plan for these formative assessments, where to find multiple-choice questions for formative assessment, and how to write your own questions, and I'll end by talking about how to revise and refine those questions.

Planning for Multiple-Choice Formative Assessment

Let's start by focusing on the formative assessment planning sheet to help you plan and organize your multiple-choice formative assessment (Table 9.1). Now that you know where you're going, let's talk about where to find questions that can help determine what students know as compared to your learning goals.

Questions From Large-Scale Assessments

Most textbooks come with test question banks; however, these questions are often not organized according to standards-based ideas, making it difficult to align the questions with your learning goals, and are of variable quality. A better place to look for questions is in the released question banks from large-scale assessments since these questions are usually carefully developed by teachers, indexed by grade level and content area, analyzed

Table 9.1 Planning Process for Multiple-Choice Formative Assessments

Step 1: Setting Learning Goals	
Science content	What common misunderstandings and prior ideas will your multiple-choice question elicit?
Supporting learning goal	What do you want students to know and be able to do?
Step 2: Finding Out What Students Know	
Assessment purpose	Will the multiple-choice question be enacted as a preassessment to find out what students know before a unit begins or as a comprehension check to monitor students' progress through the course of a unit?
Placement in unit	What is happening in the unit before and/or after the students complete the multiple-choice questions?
Assessment activity	How will multiple-choice questions be presented? Will students have their own handouts, or will questions be displayed on the board? Will the teacher collect student handouts, or will students engage in small-group or whole-class discussion?
Data to be collected about student learning	How will students' responses be aggregated to provide a representation of what the class knows? Will student response systems be used? Will data about student choices be displayed to the class or used only by the teacher?
Step 3: Anticipating Feedback	
Probable student alternative conceptions	What are the common misunderstandings, prior ideas, or misconceptions that students might have in response to this question? Are each of these represented in the distractors?
Feedback ideas	How might a unit of instruction be adapted for students who select each one of the distractors? What activities might students complete to help them integrate their prior understandings into those that are more scientifically accurate?

by statistical experts, and come with information about how students have already performed on them. Both the Trends in International Mathematics and Science Study (TIMSS) and Programme for International Student Assessment (PISA), international assessments of student learning, release large numbers of questions for public use each time they are administered, and their Web sites are good places to start writing questions. The National Assessment of Educational Progress (NAEP) also has a searchable online database of questions. Additionally, many states release multiple-choice questions from their yearly assessments online.

However, you should still review these released items with caution. Standardized-test developers tend to keep secret their best questions so they can be used over and over again. In addition, released questions are all developed for large-scale standardized tests and are not necessarily good examples of questions with distractors that will lead to useful information about student learning. This means that you'll have to carefully check the distractors to see if they are linked to your learning goals and are likely to provide you with useful information about what students know. If any one of the distractors is "I don't know" or "None of the above," Sadler (1998) suggests that these be removed, since students can pick these alternatives rather than searching for the response that best fits their own ideas.

Conceptual Inventories and Diagnostic Questions

Conceptual inventories are collections of distractor-driven multiple-choice questions focused on a particular concept. If there is a conceptual inventory already written for the content area in which you are developing a formative assessment, they will ultimately provide higher-quality information and save you time revising the question. We already examined one question that came from the Force Concept Inventory (FCI) and another from the Science Teaching Through Its Astronomical Roots (STAR) Astronomy Assessment, but these are two among of many other assessments designed specifically to get at students' common prior ideas. Other available conceptual inventories get at students' ideas about natural selection (Anderson, Fisher, & Norman, 2002), diffusion and osmosis (Odom & Barrow, 1995), and chemistry (BouJaoude, 1992). Scientists at the University of Colorado at Boulder are continuing development on a conceptual inventory of biology (Garvin-Doxas & Klymkowsky, 2008). An additional resource in physics is Jim Minstrell's DIAGNOSER project, an online portal that includes a number of questions specifically developed to *diagnose* students' understandings in physics (Thissen-Roe, Hunt, & Minstrell, 2004).

Writing Your Own Questions

If you're willing to put in a more little time, you can also create your own multiple-choice questions if you can't find any that fit your learning goals. The place to start is with the big idea question you want students to be able to answer. Then do some research on what your students might already think about this topic and develop distractors based on the students' alternative conceptions. For experienced teachers who listen closely to their students' ideas, this might be enough information. However, if you're a beginning teacher or are not as familiar with the content area in which you're writing formative assessments, doing a little research can help you anticipate what your students might say. In Chapter 4, I talked about some of the places that you can find information about students' common misconceptions, including the reference list *Students' and Teachers'*

Conceptions and Science Education (Duit, 2007), *Children's Ideas in Science* (Driver, Guesne, & Tiberghien, 1985), and the online database *Ideas Previas* (Camacho, n.d.).

After you identify students' common misconceptions about your big idea question, go ahead and assemble your question with the distractors and the scientifically accurate response. Be careful when picking your wording that the correct response is not made obvious by being a lot longer than the other alternatives or using unnecessary science vocabulary that might trigger students to guess that response. The following example illustrates this point:

> The mass of an object depends on:
>
> A. Its weight
> B. The amount of matter in it
> C. Its size
> D. Its shape

A student who didn't know the right answer to this question might easily guess *B* since it's the longest answer. Similarly, the other answers use everyday language, whereas option *B* uses more technical-sounding language. A better example is the following similar question:

> Which statement about mass is correct?
>
> A. All matter has mass.
> B. Air does not have mass.
> C. A balloon floating in air does not have mass.
> D. A floating wood block loses its mass.

All of the answers to this item use language similar in complexity, and while the responses are not exactly the same length, they are more similar than we saw in the previous item, and the longest distractor is actually not the correct answer.

Revising and Refining Multiple-Choice Questions for Formative Assessment

Once you've got a set of questions to work with, regardless of the source, take a moment to carefully read them through and decide if you've got all the elements of a good multiple-choice question; specifically, that they are linked to big ideas, are easy to understand, and include the scientifically accurate response among a set of distractors linked to students' prior ideas.

The flowchart in Figure 9.4 is based on these elements and will help you go through the process of reviewing and, if necessary, revising your questions.

HOW CAN I ENACT MULTIPLE-CHOICE QUESTIONS IN MY CLASSROOM?

As we discussed in a previous section, multiple-choice questions can be used in two different ways in your classroom for formative assessment

Figure 9.4   Flowchart for Writing Multiple-Choice Items for Formative Assessment

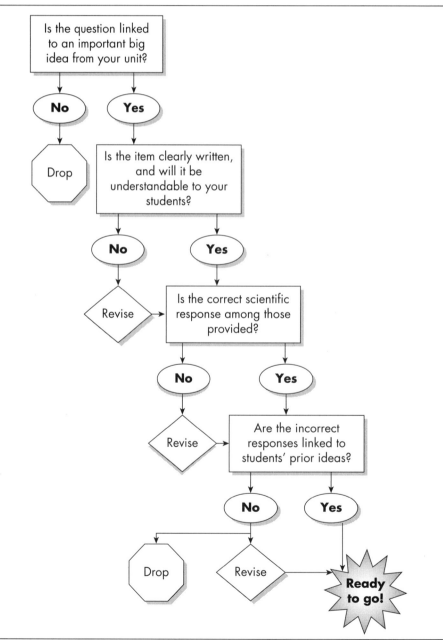

purposes: as a preassessment at the beginning of the unit or as a comprehension check after an important topic has been addressed.

For a preassessment, I suggest selecting a number of questions closely linked with the big ideas to be learned in your unit and the common alternative conceptions that go with them. A long and exhaustive collection of questions might prove overwhelming to the students and provide you with more information than you have time to interpret, so pick the best three to five questions for your preassessment. Since you'd like to find out what individual students know, ask students to respond to the questions on their own and provide space below each question for students to let you know why they chose the response they did. (See the end of this chapter for an example of how this looks.)

When you introduce the preassessment to your class, let your students know that you'll be starting a new unit, and in order to make it a more interesting and valuable learning experience, you'd like them to respond to a few questions. As always with a formative assessment, make sure that students know they will not be graded on the results. Give students a copy of the handout and then provide each of them with ample time to respond to each question. Encourage them to write as much as they can to justify their responses, and if they are not sure what to answer, ask them just to give their best guess.

Collect the handouts, and then on a blank copy of the assessment, make a quick tally of which students picked each response. This should give you a fast overview of what your class collectively knows. Pay attention to patterns of incorrect responses as you make the tally; for example, a student who consistently picks similar kinds of distractors on each question probably has a fairly solid misunderstanding of the big idea. Given this information, plan instruction to specifically incorporate what you know about the students' understandings. These steps are illustrated in Figure 9.5.

Figure 9.5 Sequence 1 for Enacting Multiple-Choice Formative Assessments

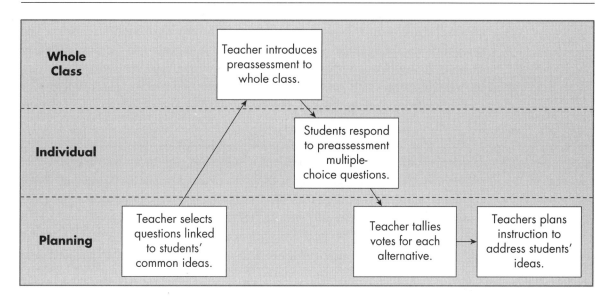

To illustrate this process more concretely, imagine that your class of 30 earth science students had responded to Sadler's question about the reasons for the seasons. The numbers to the right indicate the quantity of students who selected each distractor.

The main reason for it being hotter in summer than in winter is

A. The earth's distance from the sun changes.	15
B. The sun is higher in the sky.	5
C. The distance between the northern hemisphere and the sun changes.	8
D. Ocean currents carry warm water north.	0
E. An increase occurs in "greenhouse gases."	2

You can quickly see that although a sixth of your students already selected the correct response, *B*, half of them are coming into your class with the common prior idea that the earth is closer to the sun during the summer, *A*. A significant minority (eight) of your students think that the distance between the northern hemisphere and the sun changes, and two think it has something to do with the greenhouse effect. Therefore, when planning your lessons, you should help students to see the near equivalence in the distance between the sun and earth at different times of year (even that the earth's slightly elliptical orbit means that the earth is only slightly farther away from the sun during summer in the Northern Hemisphere), as well as to learn about the how the tilt of the earth's axis affects the angle of incidence of the sun's rays on the earth. You might even have students explain to each other how certain pictures in astronomy books might make people think the distance between the earth and sun is the reason for the seasons. The important thing is to help students make links between these prior ideas and those that are scientifically accurate.

If you are going to use a multiple-choice question as a comprehension check during a unit, I suggest taking a different approach and using the questions as starters for a whole-class conversation. The benefit of using questions this way is that during this conversation, students can share their ideas with each other and, if disagreements exist, use evidence or examples from class to argue over the strengths and weaknesses of different alternatives.

Using a multiple-choice formative assessment as a comprehension check should start with the teacher's selecting one or two questions that will really get at the main ideas that are being assessed. These questions can then be handed out to students or displayed on a projector for the class to see. It is important to allow students time to carefully read the question and think of an answer—and why they chose that answer—before holding a discussion where students share the different choices they picked and argue for or against different answers.

Once students have had ample time to think and respond, hold a vote to see what students choose as their responses. Some teachers have found it useful in middle school to have students put their heads down during this process so as not to let peer pressure impact voting. If you have the materials, asking students to hold up white boards or even vote using personal responder systems (*clickers*) can also work as a way of finding out what students know.

One good way to get the discussion started is to read out the distribution of responses ("Five students picked *A*, 10 picked *B*," and so on) and then ask for volunteers to share their reasons for each answer. Encourage students with other reasons for picking the same answer to also speak and share their thinking and reasoning. You can start by going in order of the answers, calling on students with either the least commonly chosen response or the most popular. Changing up the order each time you do this kind of formative assessment will help students to not always assume that whomever you call on is the person with the best response.

Then invite students with different responses to share their reasons and encourage them to use evidence or examples from class to support their argument. You will find that by asking multiple students to make their thinking explicit, other students in class will think about their own ideas in different ways. At the same time, you will have gained important information about what your students have learned—and what they are still struggling with—without having to take time outside of class to score or tally student responses. If the majority of students seem to have missed the main point, you should consider what you might need to reteach or revisit in upcoming activities. If there is near consensus in student responses, don't dwell on the discussion but rather make a note of the one or two students who still do not understand for individual feedback later. Figure 9.6 shows the steps described above.

An alternative to holding a whole-class conversation is to ask students to do a think-pair-share, where students first respond to the question individually, then discuss their responses in pairs before sharing their answers as a whole class. Then, in lieu of holding a whole-class conversation, you could just circulate from group to group and listen informally to discussions between students. Figure 9.7 illustrates this sequence.

Figure 9.6   Sequence 2 for Enacting Multiple-Choice Formative Assessments

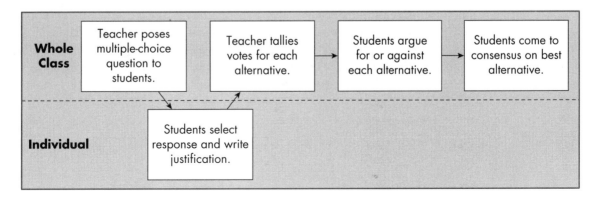

Figure 9.7   Sequence 3 for Enacting Multiple-Choice Formative Assessments

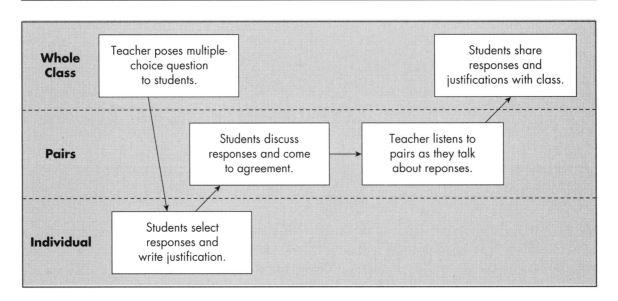

Now let's turn to some more detailed examples of what multiple-choice formative assessment looks like in the classroom, making notes and planning for appropriate follow-up.

MULTIPLE-CHOICE QUESTION EXAMPLE 9.1: UNIFORM AND NONUNIFORM MOTION

Step 1: Setting Learning Goals	
Science content	The National Science Education Standards for Motions and Forces for students in Grades 5–8 state that the motion of an object can be described by its position, direction of motion, and speed. This motion can be measured and represented on a graph.
Supporting learning goal	The students will come to know the following: • Strobe diagrams show how far the ball moved in equal amounts of time; if the distance covered by the ball is always equal, then the ball has constant velocity; if the distance covered by the ball is decreasing, then the ball has decreasing velocity. • Objects that cover the same amount of distance in the same amount of time have the same velocity.

Step 2: Finding Out What Students Know	
Assessment purpose	The purpose of this activity is to find out prior to instruction if students understand how to read strobe diagrams showing the motion of objects, as well as to determine if students have the common prior idea that objects in the same position have the same speed.
Placement in unit	Students will have had introductory experiences with observing motion and interpreting strobe diagrams for objects with uniform and nonuniform motion.
Assessment activity	Student response on handouts and whole-class discussion. The first two questions are simpler and check to see if students recognize the difference between uniform and nonuniform motion in two strobe diagrams. The third question is more challenging in that it asks students to compare the speed of two balls.
Data to be collected about student learning	First students will respond to the questions individually and justify their responses. Then the teacher will ask students to vote for the different answers they selected and ask some students to share their reasons for picking certain answers with the class. The teacher will collect these reasons under A or B on the board. The teacher will encourage students to explain their reasoning to each other to promote consensus on correct answers.
Step 3: Anticipating Feedback	
Probable student alternative conceptions	Objects at the same position have the same velocity.
Feedback ideas	Focus students on the information about the distance and time being the way to find velocity; that velocity cannot be determined by looking at only one point.

Science Content Standards are from National Research Council. (1996). *National Science Education Standards.* Washington, DC: National Academies Press, p. 154.

MULTIPLE-CHOICE QUESTIONS: UNIFORM AND NONUNIFORM MOTION

Name: _____

Date: _____ Period: _____

The strobe diagrams below show two balls moving from left to right. The letters below the diagrams represent equal points in time.

Figure 9.8 Strobe Diagram Showing Motion of Two Balls

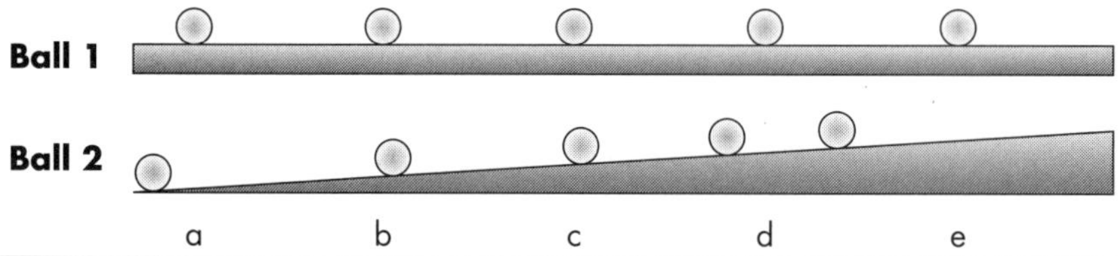

How would you describe the motion of Ball 1?

    A. Uniform
    B. Nonuniform

How do you know? _____

How would you describe the motion of Ball 2?

    A. Uniform
    B. Nonuniform

How do you know? _____

At which point on the diagram do Balls 1 and 2 have the same velocity?

    A. Exactly at point *a*
    B. Exactly at point *c*
    C. Exactly at point *d*
    D. Sometime between points *b* and *c*
    E. Sometime between points *c* and *d*

How do you know? _____

Source: Questions adapted from Trowbridge, D. E., & McDermott, L. C. (1980). Investigation of student understanding of the concept of velocity in one dimension. *American Journal of Physics, 48*(12), 1020–1028. Used with permission from the American Institute of Physics, Melville, New York.

Formative Assessment in Action: Uniform and Nonuniform Motion

During one of my research projects in Germany, I was interested to find out what seventh-grade physical science students had learned after a lesson in which they took measurements of a ball rolling on a ramp and then made graphs of its motion. Based on reading other people's research, I knew that many students have the misconception that when two objects pass each other, they have the same speed. To find out how many students still had this misconception after the lesson, I designed a formative assessment based on some research questions developed by Lillian McDermott's research group at the University of Washington (McDermott, Physics Education Group, Shaffer, & Rosenquist, 1996; Trowbridge & McDermott, 1980). I created a handout with three questions about the motion of two balls and provided space for students to justify their responses.

Since not all of these students were native English speakers, but were enrolled at an English-language international school, they often used language that a native speaker would not use to describe what they observed. I learned through the course of teaching these students the kinds of words they would use to describe uniform and nonuniform motion and anticipated those while helping them to learn the more scientific English words when I had the chance.

The day of the lesson, I brought the assessments to class and let the students know what we were going to do.

Dr. Furtak: I am going to give you a chance to show me what you learned. There's a question, and then every time you ask a question, there's a space to say how you know. Or let you tell me why you think that answer—if it is something that you learned in class, or if it was some information that's in this picture here—and then we are going to kind of talk about it, see what each other [wrote], okay? I am going to give you just a few minutes to do this.

I then gave the students about five minutes to respond to the questions, going around to individuals and responding to clarifying questions when they had them.

Dr. Furtak: What I would like to start with is just getting kind of a general idea of how you answered the first question, and I am going to ask you for your reasons why you answered it a certain way. But the first thing I want to do is to take a look to find out how many of you thought that the motion of Ball 1 was uniform, so you can just raise your hand. How many of you thought that the answer was A, uniform motion? Wow, that's everybody.

I was surprised and pleased to know that everyone in the class had correctly selected response A to the first question. However, I wanted to dig a bit deeper to learn the reason that the students had selected that answer. For that, I called on a few students to find out how they justified their responses.

Dr. Furtak: The ball has the same amount of space between each of these, okay. It's the same amount of space between each ball in the picture. What does that mean?

Peter: It means that the speed is not going up and not decreasing.

Dr. Furtak: Okay, the speed is not going up or decreasing. Okay, thank you. Anybody else? Agree or disagree?

(Continued)

(Continued)

Anna: Agree.

Dr. Furtak: Agree, okay.

At this point, I quickly glanced around the room to check the students' faces to see if anyone might be confused, but all of the students seemed comfortable with the response that had been given—essentially, that the ball in the first picture has uniform motion. I let the class know that the way Peter had described the motion of the ball could also be called uniform motion. Then, rather than ask several more students to regurgitate the same response, I made the decision to move on to the next question and to check the student handouts quickly after class to see if there were any other justifications to Question 1 that would need more attention.

I started the conversation about the next question by reminding students of their options and asking them to vote.

Dr. Furtak: Ball 2. Our options are uniform or nonuniform. Okay, how many said uniform motion? *[No students raise hands]*. Okay, nonuniform motion? *[All students raise their hands]*. Everybody. Why?

I knew right away that the majority of the students had the right idea—that the motion of the ball was nonuniform—but I still wanted to ask other students to share their reasoning this time. I asked Lena to tell us how she knew that Ball 2 had nonuniform motion.

Lena: Because the ball doesn't have the same distance to itself.

Dr. Furtak: Okay, so it does not have the same distance between itself. Not the same distance between balls.

This was an instance where Lena gave a correct explanation in a not entirely accurate phrase. Since Lena was an English language learner, I repeated what she had said and then restated it in a more scientific and grammatically correct way as I wrote it on the board. I then solicited responses from other students.

Dr. Furtak: Somebody else? What does that mean about the velocity of this ball? Yes, Tina?

Tina: It goes fastest at the bottom.

Dr. Furtak: It goes, okay, where is it fast?

Tina: At the bottom. Is it going up, or is it going down?

Dr. Furtak: Is it going up, or is it going down? Benjamin?

Benjamin: Up.

Dr. Furtak: It's going up. Let's look at the question again. Balls are going from left to right.

Benjamin: It's going up.

Dr. Furtak: Okay. So, it's going up. What does that mean, Tina?

Tina: I picked *A* because it has the most speed.

Dr. Furtak: A has the most speed? And how do you know that?

Tina: Because the space is bigger *[points to the bottom of the ramp]*, and then it gets smaller because it can't move so fast up the ramp.

In this exchange, I referred Tina's question about the direction the ball was rolling to another student, thereby getting him engaged in the conversation and checking to see if he also understood the question. By focusing on Tina telling me what it meant that the distance between the pictures of the ball was not the same, I was able to find out that she understood how to interpret the strobe diagram.

Dr. Furtak: Anybody else have an idea? Monica? We're talking about why [the ball] has uniform or nonuniform motion; why do we know that?

Monica: You say they are taking pictures between each different time, and each time the ball is released differently.

Dr. Furtak: Okay, so each time we took a picture, it's in a different place.

Monica: And it's probably going up because in the beginning it moves a lot of distance because it's just starting from the spring and then it slows down because of whatever force.

Dr. Furtak: Okay, okay, very good, thank you.

In this exchange, I found out that Monica was already moving beyond just interpreting the strobe diagrams to thinking about the reason that the ball slowed down when it rolled up the ramp.

To this point, there had not been disagreement between students' responses, but I anticipated there would be more conversation about Question 3 since this was the question designed to elicit students' alternative conception that the balls would have the same velocity when they were at the same place on the diagram. I chose to start the discussion with a think-pair-share.

Dr. Furtak: Question 3 is more tricky. At which point on the diagram do Balls 1 and 2 have the same velocity? I want you to turn to the person next to you and tell them what you answered and see if they have the same answer as you.

Students turned to each other and chatted loudly for a minute or two. When the talking quieted down, several students tried to catch my attention so they could tell the class what they thought.

Dr. Furtak: You really want to tell me the answer? That's great because I want to hear it. What I would like to do is have one person from each group just tell me what answer you picked and why.

The first pair that shared their ideas correctly identified the space between points b and c as being the place where the balls had the same velocity. One of these students, Victor, came to the front of the room and labeled the diagram so that we could all see which spaces he was talking about. The next pair agreed with the first pair's answer, giving the reason that during the time between points b and c, the balls had covered almost equal distance in equal time.

The disagreement came when I called on the next pair.

Kirsten: We think it's, well, we're still debating between at point c and between points d and c.

Dr. Furtak: Okay, so you are saying it might be, so give me the argument first for answer C.

(Continued)

(Continued)

Kirsten:	For answer *C*? The reasons seem to be the speed of the balls should be the same because they are lined up exactly. And then on the other one, well, the balls aren't exactly like, they aren't exactly, but they are very close. So, I don't know, if we are doing very precise science here, then it would be answer *D*, but we are just people in the class, and it's point *c*.
Dr. Furtak:	Can we do both? Can we be both precise scientists and people in this class?
Kirsten:	Uh, okay, yeah.

After taking the opportunity to remind Kirsten that we could be both scientists and students at the same time, I decided to ask another group to directly address Kristen's group.

Dr. Furtak:	So this is really interesting. So we have these reasons for answer *C*, and three reasons for answer *D*. I would like to hear someone who gave me one of these answers tell Kirsten's group why do you think it's *D*?
Nick:	It can't be *D* because they are not exactly at the same height [at point *b*]. If it's at the same height, it doesn't matter.
Dr. Furtak:	Okay, you are saying, what do you mean it doesn't matter? Do you want to come up and show me what you mean? Come on up and draw it on the board.

I had a feeling that when Nick said the balls were not exactly at the same height, he meant that the balls were not exactly at the same position, and that this didn't matter. By asking him to come to the board, the students and I were quickly able to understand that he was substituting the word *height* for *position*.

Nick:	[Drawing] Because it doesn't matter if these points are at the same time. Same space matters.
Dr. Furtak:	You are saying that the space is more important than the position.

By repeating what Nick had said while using the term *position* instead of *height*, I was able to check that I had understood him correctly, while at the same time reinforcing his use of the correct word to describe his idea.

While Nick was at the board, some students were speaking animatedly to each other at the back of the class. I called on one of those students to share what he was thinking.

Eric:	Actually, even at point *c*, at that one they are not perfectly aligned.
Dr. Furtak:	They are, or they are not?
Eric:	They are not.
Dr. Furtak:	They are not. So let's um, if they were perfectly aligned, does that mean they were going the same velocity?
Eric:	No.

I took the opportunity with Eric to move him away from the concern that the balls were not perfectly aligned and push him to state that even if the balls were aligned, that would not mean they had the same velocity. Then, I called on Lisa, who had been shaking her head *no* while Eric was talking.

Lisa: Well, because as the boys in the back row just said, I actually fully believe that the space in between matches more…

Dr. Furtak: You can't tell how fast they are going from what?

Lisa: You can't tell how fast they are going just from the, at the points because you don't know; I don't know how to explain it.

Dr. Furtak: Okay. That's good thinking. Sam, you had something?

Lisa had the right idea but struggled to put it into words. I gave her some feedback that she was doing good thinking and then called on Sam, who was able to explain Lisa's ideas more clearly.

Sam: Well, as all of you may think, it would also be velocity and speed, and speed can be measured by the position of the ball. And so if they can be in the same position as the one that is overtaking, it would be like overtaking another car. It looks like you're at the same place, but then you are away again because you have more speed.

Dr. Furtak: Oh, that's an interesting idea.

Sam: That's why C can't be, because one is going up, and the other is slowing down.

Lisa: Yeah, like if you freeze them, one of them would be faster than the other.

While there had initially been some disagreement about the right choice, several different students had spoken about the reason why it was more important to focus on the space that the balls had covered in an amount of time, rather than at the position of two balls at an instant in time.

I decided at that point not to force the students to vote again and to follow up with some of the students who had the incorrect idea individually after class. I thanked the group for their enthusiastic participation, feeling confident that the formative assessment had helped me to find out what they were thinking and had helped them to clarify their ideas and talk with each other about them.

In reflecting on the experience, I can see ways I will adapt the way I use the formative assessment with students next time. I could have started with a think-pair-share where the *think* phase was when students responded to the assessment in writing, and the *pair* phase had students speaking with each other about what they wrote, so that the *share* would have been a richer discussion with more participants. I could have displayed a picture of the diagram on the board so that students could draw on it while they had their discussion to illustrate their points. Overall, I still believe the assessment was a learning opportunity for me and for the students and will influence the way I enact formative assessments in the future.

MULTIPLE-CHOICE QUESTION EXAMPLE 9.2: DIFFUSION

Step 1: Setting Learning Goals	
Science content	The Grades 9–12 National Science Education Standards for Life Sciences state that students should know that cells have particular structures that underlie their functions. Every cell is surrounded by a membrane that separates it from the outside world. Inside the cell is a concentrated mixture of thousands of different molecules that form a variety of specialized structures that carry out such cell functions as energy production, transport of molecules, waste disposal, synthesis of new molecules, and the storage of genetic material.
Supporting learning goal	The students will come to know how changes in concentration of molecules on either side of a membrane can affect the net flow of molecules from one side to the other. Actual net flux is a result of random processes (molecular movements) and probabilities.
Step 2: Finding Out What Students Know	
Assessment purpose	To determine if students understand that the difference in concentration determines how quickly molecules move from areas of high to low concentration.
Placement in unit	After an introduction to the concepts of concentration and diffusion, this formative assessment is designed to elicit alternative conceptions about the random motion of molecules.
Assessment activity	Working with one question at a time, ask students to vote on the first question and then display the diagram on the board. Invite students to use the diagram to explain their answer to Question 1. Then ask students to vote on their answers to Question 1 and use the diagram as an opportunity to discuss the students' responses.
Data to be collected about student learning	Tally the number of students who chose each response and informally keep track of the arguments students give to support the different responses.
Step 3: Anticipating Feedback	
Probable student alternative conceptions	Students often think that molecules *want* to move from areas of high to low concentrations, and that the diffusion rate is the same regardless of the difference in concentration (Meir, Perry, Stal, Maruca, & Klopfer, 2005). Students are likely to indicate on the diagram that the molecules will move in the direction of lower concentration rather than showing that any of the molecules could move in any direction at any given moment in time.
Feedback ideas	Remind students that molecules do not *want* to move but move as a result of random processes. This can be indicated on the diagram by multiple arrows coming from each individual molecule pointing in every possible direction (Meir, Perry, Stal, Maruca, & Klopfer, 2005). Tell students that rather than individual molecules going from high to low concentration, it is the ensemble of molecules that displays a net flux from high to low concentration.

Science Content Standards are from National Research Council. (1996). *National Science Education Standards.* Washington, DC: National Academies Press.

MULTIPLE-CHOICE QUESTIONS: DIFFUSION

Name: _____

Date: _____ Period: _____

Instructions: For each of the following questions, select what you believe is the best answer and then pick the statement that best describes why you think so.

1. As the difference in concentration between two areas increases, the rate of diffusion (net flux)

   A. Decreases
   B. Increases

2. Illustrate your answer by drawing arrows on the diagram below indicating in which direction molecules would be likely to move in the next instant of time.

Figure 9.9 Diffusion Diagram

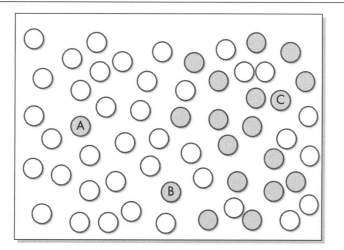

3. Why do you think this would happen?

   A. There is less room for the particles to move.
   B. If the concentration is high enough, the particles will spread less, and the rate will be slowed.
   C. The molecules want to spread out.
   D. The greater likelihood of random motion into other regions.

Source: Questions 1 and 3 from Odom, A. L., & Kelly, P. V. (2001). Integrating concept mapping and the learning cycle to teach diffusion and osmosis concepts to high school biology students. *Science Education, 85,* 615–635. Used with permission from John Wiley and Sons, Inc., Hoboken, New Jersey. Question 2 adapted from Meir, E., Perry, J., Stal, D., Maruca, S., & Klopfer, E. (2005). How effective are simulated molecular-level experiments for teaching diffusion and osmosis? *Cell Biology Education, 4,* 235–248. Copyright © 2005 by American Society for Cell Biology.

Resources

This section is intended to provide you with additional resources as you go through the formative assessment process. You can use these blank planning sheets to develop your own formative assessments, starting with standards or a curriculum and working through the five different types of assessments discussed in this book. The following planning sheets are included:

A. Setting Learning Goals: Working From Standards

B. Setting Learning Goals: Starting From a Curriculum

C. From Learning Goals to Feedback

D. Big Ideas Question

E. Concept Maps

F. Predict-Observe-Explain

G. Evidence-to-Explanation

H. Multiple-Choice Questions

Planning Sheet A

Setting Learning Goals: Working From Standards

Step 1: Identify Standard(s) for the Unit

Science Content:

Step 2: Unpack Standard Into Goals and Big Idea Question for Unit

Learning Goal	*Big Idea Question*

Step 3: Write Supporting Goals for Unit

The students will be able to do/come to know the following:	
1	
2	
3	
4	

Planning Sheet B

Setting Learning Goals: Starting From a Curriculum

Step 1: Unit Summary

Activity Title	Student Activities	Learning Goal

Step 2: Overarching Unit Goal and Big Idea Question

Unit Goal	Big Idea Question

Step 3a: Prioritize Learning Goals

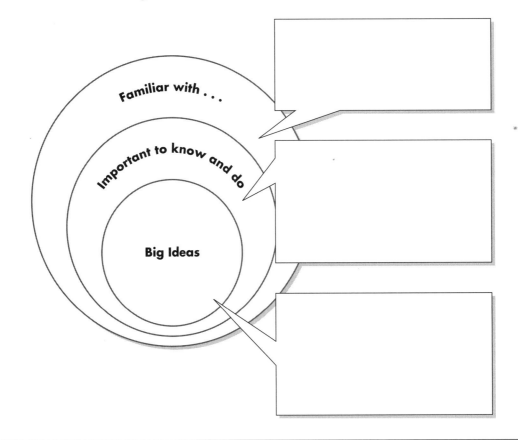

Source: Adapted with permission from *Understanding by Design* (2nd ed., p. 71) by Grant Wiggins and Jay McTighe. Alexandria, VA: ASCD. © 2005 by ASCD. Used with permission. Learn more about ASCD at www.ascd.org.

Step 3b: Write Supporting Learning Goals for Unit

The students will be able to do/come to know the following:	
1	
2	
3	
4	

Planning Sheet C

From Learning Goals to Feedback

Step 1: Setting Learning Goals	
Science content	
Overarching learning goal	
Big idea question	
Supporting learning goal	
Step 2: Finding Out What Students Know	
Assessment purpose	
Placement in unit	
Assessment activity	
Data to be collected about student learning	
Step 3: Anticipating Feedback	
Probable student alternative conceptions	
Feedback ideas	

Planning Sheet D

Big Ideas Question

Step 1: Setting Learning Goals	
Science content	What standards-based understanding will your big idea be based on? What is the big idea that your unit is addressing?
Supporting learning goal	What is the scientific explanation that you expect students to provide in response to the big idea question? What evidence and/or examples will you consider to be acceptable in response to this question?
Step 2: Finding Out What Students Know	
Assessment purpose	How will students respond to the big idea question at this point in the unit? How do they support their answer with evidence and examples learned in class?
Placement in unit	How far into the unit will you wait before asking students to respond to the big idea question for the first time? How often will you revisit the question?
Assessment activity	Will students work individually or in a small group? If students are working in a small group, should they collect all the different answers that they have within the group or come to a consensus? Will there be a whole-class conversation in which students share and defend their ideas?
Data to be collected about student learning	How will you categorize students' different responses? Will you read through all of their individual responses, or will you listen to what they present to the whole class?
Step 3: Anticipating Feedback	
Probable student alternative conceptions	What common prior ideas and misunderstandings do you expect students to express in response to the question? What elements of the question do you anticipate students will not yet understand? What prior experiences or everyday examples from outside of class do you expect them to share?
Feedback ideas	How can you help students focus on the evidence and examples studied in class to support their conclusions? How can you help them explain their prior ideas through the lens of the acceptable scientific explanation?

Planning Sheet E

Concept Maps

Step 1: Setting Learning Goals	
Science content	What standard will you be addressing with the formative assessment?
Supporting learning goal	What are the important concepts that students will come to know?
Step 2: Finding Out What Students Know	
Assessment purpose	Why do students need to be able to relate these particular terms? What propositions between terms do you want them to be able to make?
Placement in unit	Will students know all of the concept terms when they work on the map or only some? Will students complete the concept map only once or multiple times as they progress through the unit?
Assessment activity	Will students work on their maps only individually or also in small groups? Will you hold a discussion about connecting key concept terms after they have worked on their own?
Data to be collected about student learning	Will you look at individual maps or group maps? What kinds of conversations will you be looking for as students are working in groups?
Step 3: Anticipating Feedback	
Probable student alternative conceptions	Which concept terms do you expect students will have more trouble connecting with the others? What are the common misunderstandings, prior beliefs, or misconceptions that might be exposed in students' propositions?
Feedback ideas	How can you help students to relate *orphan* concept terms with ones they already understand? How might you help students with incorrect propositions make more accurate connections?

Planning Sheet F

Predict-Observe-Explain

Step 1: Setting Learning Goals	
Science content	What standards-based understandings will your POE address? Think not only about content-based standards but also about which understandings about inquiry that the activity might target.
Supporting learning goal	What do you want students to know and be able to do?
Step 2: Finding Out What Students Know	
Assessment purpose	What is the purpose of this activity, and why is it being placed at this point in the unit?
Placement in unit	What is happening in the unit before and after the students complete the POE?
Assessment activity	What exactly will be demonstrated? What information will students be given before they make their predictions? What exactly will students predict?
Data to be collected about student learning	How will the students share their understanding: through a vote, by sharing ideas at tables before sharing with the whole class, or in a whole-class discussion where students volunteer their answers?
Step 3: Anticipating Feedback	
Probable student alternative conceptions	What are the common misunderstandings, prior beliefs, or misconceptions that students might draw on?
Feedback ideas	What activities might students complete to help them see that their prior understandings are not as accurate as the scientific explanation you expect them to reach?

Planning Sheet G

Evidence-to-Explanation

Step 1: Setting Learning Goals	
Science content	What standard will you be addressing with the formative assessment?
Supporting learning goal	What standards-based conceptual understandings are you trying to assess? What kind of evidence (figure, table, or graph) is both a good representation of the content and a basis for asking an explanation-type question?
Step 2: Finding Out What Students Know	
Assessment purpose	What is the purpose of having students interpret this graph?
Placement in unit	What is happening in the unit before and after the students complete the evidence-to-explanation assessment?
Assessment activity	What is the nature of the data that will be included in the graph? Will students have seen this graph or one like it before, or will it be completely new to them? What information needs to accompany the graph in order for students to interpret it? What it the interpretation that you are looking for?
Data to be collected about student learning	Once students have interpreted the graph and provided an explanation, how will they demonstrate their understanding to you?
Step 3: Anticipating Feedback	
Probable student alternative conceptions	In what ways might students misinterpret or misunderstand the evidence? What are the common misunderstandings, prior beliefs, or alternative conceptions that students might use to explain the evidence?
Feedback ideas	What activities might help students develop the conceptual understanding necessary to provide the correct explanation for the evidence they have been given?

Planning Sheet H

Multiple-Choice Questions

Step 1: Setting Learning Goals	
Science content	What common misunderstandings and prior ideas will your multiple-choice question elicit?
Supporting learning goal	What do you want students to know and be able to do?
Step 2: Finding Out What Students Know	
Assessment purpose	Will the multiple-choice question be enacted as a preassessment to find out what students know before a unit begins or as a comprehension check to monitor students' progress through the course of a unit?
Placement in unit	What is happening in the unit before and/or after the students complete the multiple-choice questions?
Assessment activity	How will multiple-choice questions be presented: will students have their own handouts, or will questions be displayed on the board? Will the teacher collect student handouts, or will students engage in small-group or whole-class discussion?
Data to be collected about student learning	How will students' responses be aggregated to provide a representation of what the class knows? Will student-response systems be used? Will data about student choices be displayed to the class or used only by the teacher?
Step 3: Anticipating Feedback	
Probable student alternative conceptions	What are the common misunderstandings, prior ideas, or misconceptions that students might have in response to this question? Are each of these represented in the distractors?
Feedback ideas	How might a unit of instruction be adapted for students who select each one of the distractors? What activities might students complete to help them integrate their prior understandings into those that are more scientifically accurate?

Glossary

Alternative conceptions   Student ideas about the natural world that are based on prior experiences or misunderstandings about science.

Authentic questions   Questions that are genuine requests for information that the teacher could not have answered himself or herself (Cazden, 2001)—for example, asking a student where he or she was born.

Backward planning   Wiggins and McTighe's (2005) planning process that starts with unpacking standards into learning goals, determining what will be acceptable evidence that students have reached those learning goals, organizing those goals according to their level of importance, and then planning activities that will build the understanding represented in that final goal.

Big idea assessments   Formative assessment in which students respond to the big idea question for the unit.

Big idea question   A question based on the unifying themes of science that can frame the overarching learning goal for a unit.

Big ideas   General, unifying ideas in science that can orient students' inquiries into a unit.

Class survey   Instructional strategy in which the teacher asks students to share a selection of their ideas with the whole class.

Comprehension check   A formative assessment performed in the middle of the unit to "check" to see if students have comprehended a particular concept.

Concept map   A graphical representation of the relationship between concept terms.

Conceptual inventory   A type of assessment specifically designed to assess students' understanding of a conceptual domain, with a focus on identifying students' prior ideas and misconceptions—for example, the Force Concept Inventory (Hestenes, Wells, & Swackhammer, 1992).

Declarative knowledge   Knowing *what*—for example, facts and definitions.

Discrepant event   An event that has an unexpected outcome and can help students see that their scientific ideas are not enough to explain a given natural phenomenon.

Distractors Alternative responses to multiple-choice questions that are linked to students' common ideas.

Evidence-to-explanation assessment Formative assessment in which students are asked to interpret some form of evidence, such as a graph, diagram, or figure, and to develop an explanation based on that evidence.

Feedback Information provided to the learner about how to improve his or her performance.

Formative assessment Process of assessment that takes place while learning is in progress to inform teaching and learning so that students will meet learning goals.

Formative assessment loop Three-step process in which the teacher sets a learning goal, determines what the student knows with respect to that goal, and then provides feedback to help students reach the learning goal (same as *feedback loop*).

Inquiry-based curricula Curricula derived from an inquiry-based approach in which students learn by engaging in the thinking processes and activities of scientists.

Instructional questions Questions to which the teacher already knows the answers and that are asked only for the purpose of instruction.

IRE A pattern of classroom interaction in which the teacher *initiates* a question, the student *responds*, and the teacher *evaluates* the student's response (Mehan, 1979).

Jigsaw and debate An activity in which students are placed in different *expert* groups that focus on a particular topic for discussion, then are split up into new groups with an expert from each original group.

Learning goal Statements of what your students will know and be able to do as a result of an activity, lesson, unit, or course.

Learning progression A map of student ideas with students' prior ideas and alternative conceptions on one end, the overarching learning goal on the other, and the supporting learning goals in the middle.

Multiple-choice questions Questions with a set of possible responses to which students can select the answer they believe best addresses the question.

NAEP National Assessment of Educational Progress—A standardized assessment administered by the Department of Education to a nationwide sample of 4th-, 8th-, and 12th-grade students.

Open-ended questions Questions that begin with *how* or *why* so that students cannot give *one-word* or *yes* or *no* answers.

Open response Assessment with an unconstrained space in which students can write their responses.

Overarching goal   Main goal for a unit of instruction or course of study.

Peer review   Process in which students review each other's work and compare it to some kind of criterion, such as learning goals or exemplars.

PISA   Programme for International Student Assessment—An international standardized assessment administered by the Organization for Economic Cooperation and Development (OECD) to 15-year-olds in participating countries.

Predict-observe-explain assessment   Formative assessment in which students *predict* what will happen in a given experimental setting, *observe* what actually happens, and then *explain* why what they observed happened (White & Gunstone, 1992).

Procedural knowledge   Knowing *how* to do something—for example, making a graph.

Real questions   Questions to which the teacher does not already know the answer and are thus genuine requests for information; same as *authentic* questions.

Schematic knowledge   Knowing *why* something happens—for example, why it's warmer in the summer than in the winter.

Self-review   Instructional strategy in which students evaluate their own work based on an answer key or exemplar.

Summative assessment   Assessment that's intended to take place when instruction is finished to establish what students have learned.

Supporting goals   Learning goals that build on each other toward an overarching learning goal, usually written for a lesson or series of lessons.

Table conference   Instructional strategy in which students share their explanations with their small group.

Table consensus   Instructional strategy in which students share their explanation with their small group and then argue those explanations on the basis of evidence to come to a consensus on the best explanation.

Think-pair-share   Instructional strategy in which students are given time to silently *think* about their response to a question; they then *pair* with another student to discuss their response and then *share* their response with the whole class.

TIMSS   Trends in International Mathematics and Science Study—An international standardized assessment administered by the International Association for the Evaluation of Educational Achievement (IEA) to fourth- and eighth-grade students in participating countries.

References

American Association for the Advancement of Science. (1990). *Science for all Americans*. New York: Oxford University Press.

American Association for the Advancement of Science. (1993). *Benchmarks for science literacy*. New York: Oxford University Press.

American Chemical Society. (2007). *Inquiry in action: Investigating matter through inquiry* (3rd ed.). Washington, DC: American Chemical Society.

Anderson, D. L., Fisher, K. M., & Norman, G. J. (2002). Development and evaluation of the conceptual inventory of natural selection. *Journal of Research in Science Teaching, 39*(10), 952–978.

Ayala, C. C., Shavelson, R. J., Ruiz-Primo, M. A., Brandon, P., Yin, Y., Furtak, E. M., et al. (2008). From formal embedded assessments to reflective lessons: The development of formative assessment suites. *Applied Measurement in Education, 21*(4), 315–334.

Biological Sciences Curriculum Study. (2006). *BSCS biology: An ecological approach* (10th ed.). Dubuque, IA: Kendall/Hunt.

Black, P. (1998). Assessment by teachers and the improvement of students' Learning. In B. J. Fraser & K. G. Tobin (Eds.), *International handbook of science education* (pp. 811–822). Dordrecht, Netherlands: Kluwer Academic Publishers.

Black, P., & Wiliam, D. (1998). Assessment and classroom learning. *Assessment in Education, 5*(1), 7–74.

Borsese, A., Lumbaca, P., & Pentimalli, R. (1996). Investigacion sobre las concepciones de los estudiantes acerca de los estado de agregacion y los cambios de estado [Investigation of student conceptions about the states of aggregation and the changes of state. Teaching of the Sciences]. *Ensenanza de las Ciencias, 14*(1), 15–24.

BouJaoude, S. B. (1992). The relationship between students' learning strategies and the change in their misunderstandings during a high school chemistry course. *Journal of Research in Science Teaching, 29*(7), 687–699.

Butler, R. (1987). Task-involving and ego-involving properties of evaluation: Effects of different feedback conditions on motivational perceptions, interest, and performance. *Journal of Educational Psychology, 79*(4), 474–482.

Butler, R., & Nisan, M. (1986). Effects of no feedback, task-related comments, and grades on intrinsic motivation and performance. *Journal of Educational Psychology, 78*(3), 210–216.

Camacho, F. F. (n.d.). Ideas previas. Retrieved June 10, 2008, from http://ideasprevias.cinstrum.unam.mx:2048/presentation.htm

Cazden, C. B. (2001). *Classroom discourse: The language of teaching and learning*. Portsmouth, NH: Heinemann.

Chi, M. T. H., Glaser, R., & Far, M. J. (1988). *The nature of expertise*. Hillsdale, NJ: Lawrence Erlbaum.

Cohen, E. G. (1994). *Designing groupwork* (2nd ed.). New York: Teachers College Press.

Driver, R., Guesne, E., & Tiberghien, A. (1985). *Children's ideas in science*. Philadelphia: Open University Press.

Duit, R. (2007). Students' and teachers' conceptions and science education (Publication). Retrieved June 10, 2008, from http://www.ipn.uni-kiel.de/aktuell/stcse/stcse.html

Duschl, R. A. (2003). Assessment of inquiry. In J. M. Atkin & J. Coffey (Eds.), *Everyday assessment in the science classroom* (pp. 41–59). Arlington, VA: NSTA Press.

Furtak, E. M., & Ruiz-Primo, M.A. (2007). *Effectiveness of four types of formative assessment prompts in providing information about students' understanding in writing and in discussions*. Paper presented at the American Educational Research Association Annual Conference, Chicago, Illinois.

Furtak, E. M., & Ruiz-Primo, M. A. (2008). Making students' thinking explicit in writing and discussion: An analysis of formative assessment prompts. *Science Education, 92,* 799–824.

Garvin-Doxas, K., & Klymkowsky, M. (2008). Understanding randomness and its impact on student learning: Lessons learned from building the biology concept inventory (BCI). *Life Sciences Education, 7*(2), 227–233.

Harlow, D., & Otero, V. (2005). Collaboration physics: Elementary teachers and university researchers join forces to help students construct understanding of friction—and discover something of the nature of science in the process. *Science & Children, 42*(5), 35–39.

Hattie, J., & Timperley, H. (2007). The power of feedback. *Review of Educational Research, 77*(1), 81–112.

Hestenes, D., Wells, M., & Swackhamer, G. (1992). Force concept inventory. *The Physics Teacher, 30*(3), 141–151.

Lawrence Hall of Science. (2000). *Variables.* Nashua, NH: Delta Education.

Li, M., Ruiz-Primo, M. A., & Shavelson, R. J. (2006). Towards a science achievement framework: The case of TIMSS-R study. In T. Plomp & S. Howie (Eds.), *Contexts of learning mathematics and science: Lessons learned from TIMSS* (pp. 291–312). New York: Routledge.

McDermott, L. C., Physics Education Group, U. of W., Shaffer, P. S., & Rosenquist, M. L. (1996). *Physics by inquiry: An introduction to physics and the physical sciences, Vol. 2.* New York: John Wiley & Sons.

Mehan, H. (1979). *Learning lessons.* Cambridge, MA: Harvard University Press.

Meir, E., Perry, J., Stal, D., Maruca, S., & Klopfer, E. (2005). How effective are simulated molecular-level experiments for teaching diffusion and osmosis? *Cell Biology Education, 4,* 235–248.

National Center for Education Statistics. (2007). NAEP Questions (Publication) Retrieved June 10, 2008, from http://nces.ed.gov/nationsreportcard/itmrls/startsearch.asp

National Center for Education Statistics. (2008). Trends in international mathematics and science study: Released items [Electronic Version]. Retrieved June 9, 2008, from http://nces.ed.gov/TIMSS/Educators.asp

National Research Council. (1996). *National science education standards.* National Academies Press.

National Research Council. (2001). *Classroom assessment and the national science education standards.* Washington, D.C.: National Academies Press.

National Research Council. (2007). *Taking science to school: learning and teaching science in grades K-8.* Washington, D.C.: National Academies Press.

Odom, A. L., & Barrow, L. H. (1995). Development and application of a two-tier diagnostic test measuring college biology students' understanding of diffusion and osmosis after a course of instruction. *Journal of Research in Science Teaching, 32*(1), 45–61.

Pottenger, F. M., & Young, D. B. (1992). *The local environment: FAST 1. Foundational approaches to science teaching* (2nd ed.). Honolulu: Curriculum Research and Development Group.

Reeve, J., & Jang, H. (2006). What teachers say and do to support students' autonomy during a learning activity. *Journal of Educational Psychology, 98*(1), 209–218.

Ross, K. E. K., & Shuell, T. J. (1990). *The earthquake information test: Validating an instrument for determining student misconceptions.* Paper presented at the Annual Meeting of the Northeastern Educational Research Association, Ellenville, NY, October 31–November 2, 1990.

Rudolph, J. L., & Stewart, J. (1998). Evolution and the nature of science: On the historical discord and its implications for science education. *Journal of Research in Science Teaching, 35*(10), 1069–1089.

Ruiz-Primo, M. A., & Furtak, E. M. (2004). *Informal assessment of students' understanding of scientific inquiry.* Paper presented at the American Educational Research Association Annual Conference, San Diego, CA.

Sadler, D. R. (1989). Formative assessment and the design of instructional systems. *Instructional Science, 18*, 119–144.

Sadler, P. M. (1998). Psychometric models of student conceptions in science: Reconciling qualitative studies and distractor-driven assessment instruments. *Journal of Research in Science Teaching, 35*(3), 265–296.

Seidel, T., Rimmele, R., & Prenzel, M. (2005). Clarity and coherence of lesson goals as a scaffold for student learning. *Learning and Instruction, 15*(6), 539–556.

Smith, J. P., diSessa, A. A., & Roschelle, J. (1993). Misconceptions reconceived: A constructivist analysis of knowledge in transition. *The Journal of the Learning Sciences, 3*(2), 115–163.

Stanford Education Assessment Laboratory. (2003). *Teacher's guide to the reflective lessons.* Unpublished manuscript.

Stefanou, C. R., Perencevich, K. C., DiCintio, M., & Turner, J. C. (2004). Supporting autonomy in the classroom: Ways teachers encourage student decision making and ownership. *Educational Psychologist, 39*(2), 97–110.

Thissen-Roe, A., Hunt, E., & Minstrell, J. (2004). The DIAGNOSER project: Combining assessment and learning. *Behavior Research Methods, Instruments, and Computers, 36*(2), 234–240.

Trowbridge, D. E., & McDermott, L. C. (1980). Investigation of student understanding of the concept of velocity in one dimension. *American Journal of Physics, 48*(12), 1020–1028.

Vanides, J., Yin, Y., Tomita, M., & Ruiz-Primo, M. A. (2005). Using concept maps in the science classroom. *Science Scope, 28*(8), 27–31.

White, B. Y., & Frederiksen, J. R. (1998). Inquiry, modeling, and metacognition: Making science accessible to all students. *Cognition and Instruction, 16*(1), 3–118.

White, R., & Gunstone, R. (1992). *Probing understanding.* New York: Falmer.

Wiggins, G., & McTighe, J. (2005). *Understanding by design* (2nd ed.). Alexandria, VA: Association for Supervision and Curriculum Development.

Wiliam, D. (2007). Keeping learning on track: Classroom assessment and the regulation of learning. In F. K. Lester Jr. (Ed.), *Second handbook of mathematics teaching and learning* (pp. 1053–1098). Greenwich, CT: Information Age Publishing.

Index

CORWIN

A SAGE Company